THE
FRENCH & INDIAN
WAR IN
NORTH CAROLINA

THE
FRENCH & INDIAN
WAR IN
NORTH CAROLINA

THE SPREADING FLAMES OF WAR

JOHN R. MAASS

Charleston · London

THE
History
PRESS

Published by The History Press
Charleston, SC 29403
www.historypress.net

Front cover: *Fort Dobbs* by Robert G. Steele.

First published 2013

Manufactured in the United States

ISBN 978.1.60949.887.0

Library of Congress CIP data applied for.

This book is dedicated to Molly, Eileen and Charlie Maass and to the memory of my parents, Richard and Peggy Maass.

CONTENTS

ACKNOWLEDGEMENTS

Many people helped me to write this book, and I would be remiss not to thank them for the kindly assistance they provided to me in the process of my research and writing. Robert M. Calhoon was my graduate advisor from 1999–2002, when I began the research and writing on North Carolina during the French and Indian War, and has been steadfastly encouraging me to pursue it ever since. Scott Douglas of Fort Dobbs State Historic Site answered my many questions, read the manuscript, helped me work through some historical problems and was an enthusiastic supporter of this project from its inception. Lawrence E. Babits, professor emeritus at East Carolina University, made helpful suggestions and comments on the manuscript, particularly those concerning Fort Dobbs. Daniel J. Totora reviewed a portion of the manuscript and answered my inquiries pertaining to the Cherokee War. His time, comments and suggestions were invaluable to me, particularly regarding the sites of the battles and towns associated with this part of the conflict. Likewise, Joshua Howard assisted with his extensive knowledge of early North Carolina history to my great benefit. Thanks go to Robert G. Steele for the use of his striking conjectural image of Fort Dobbs and to Erik Goldstein of Colonial Williamsburg for assisting with images of maps, weapons and currency. Ellen Kutcher gave her time to me at Historic Bethabara for a tour, and Gennifer L. Reiter, manager of Fort Dobbs State Historic Site, was invaluable in her efforts to procure images for the book.

For their generous efforts on my behalf, I also thank Scott L. Lance, James Rogers Jr., William Jack, Mathew Waehner, Jason Melius, Barbara

Lombardi, Kim Anderson, Christine I. Wilbanks, Jim Mullins, Todd Post, Olaf Nippe, Keith Longiotti, Todd Hostetter, Hillary S. Kativa, Jeffrey P. Oves, Anne Miller, Donna E. Kelly, Susan M. Trimble, Greg Jones, Charles B. Baxley, Johnny Vitorovich, George Bray, Doug Raines, Tim Cutler, James C. Kelly, David Miller, John Ferling, Annie Urban, Ellen M. Clark, Marianne Martin, Beth Hill, Rich Strum, Erik Villard, Shannon Walker, James Piecuch and Karen Ipock.

Last but surely not least, my gratitude goes to Banks Smither and Julia Turner at The History Press, for their support for this project and encouragement along the way.

INTRODUCTION

Most Americans know little, if anything, about the French and Indian War. Schoolchildren today are largely ignorant of this conflict, also called the Seven Years' War, since knowledge of its history is not required on the standardized tests many of them take or the "standards of learning" most are required to master. General readers of United States history will usually recognize the war's name and perhaps even guess that it occurred during the American colonial period, but most likely, they will recall it as "a kind of hazy backdrop to the Revolution" and "little more than a footnote," in the words of noted historian Fred Anderson. When it happened and who fought whom are also questions that would no doubt stump the vast majority of Americans if asked.[1]

Most people who have heard of the war, have read about it or have visited historic sites related to its events, and even many who consider themselves to be French and Indian War "buffs," know only about the northern theater of the war. Places such as Fort Ticonderoga and the Plains of Abraham at Quebec are quite familiar to these enthusiasts, and many will also have visited or read about Fortress Louisbourg in Nova Scotia, Crown Point in New York and Fort William Henry on Lake George—the latter associated with the events described in *The Last of the Mohicans* and the many films and television productions based on James Fenimore Cooper's 1826 novel. Moreover, almost all the famous figures associated with the war served at these northern places—particularly Montcalm and Wolfe, as well as Major Robert Rogers of the famous ranger battalion he led.

There has been little attention paid to the southern area of operations during the French and Indian War or the wartime contributions of the southern colonies in contrast to the notoriety of the conflict's battles and leaders in the northern theater—Canada and New York for the most part. When I began my research into North Carolina during this little-known conflict as part of the requirements for a master's degree in history, the overwhelming response from people who asked me what I was studying was some variation of "I didn't know there was anything to do with the French and Indian War in the South." I heard this even from professional military and colonial historians, who assumed that this colonial struggle was waged exclusively "up north." This is not surprising in that almost all histories of the war ignore the South, particularly North Carolina. Even the great French philosopher and historian of the Enlightenment Voltaire summed up the war in 1758 as merely a "war about a few acres of snow somewhere around Canada."[2]

These responses validated my choice of a research topic, since little modern scholarship had been completed on the Tar Heel State's participation in the war and because of a renewed interest in the pre-Revolutionary conflict by the early 2000s. Much of this new popular and academic enthusiasm for this subject area—including my own—can be attributed to the publication in 2000 of Fred Anderson's *The Crucible of War: The Seven Years' War and the Fate of Empire in British North America, 1754–1766*, the definitive history of these hostilities, which blends a wonderful accessibility for general readers with solid research to satisfy "scholarly expectations." Unlike the majority of general histories of the war, which often fail to mention the South or its contributions to the war effort at all, Anderson provided an excellent overview of southern campaigns, operations and leaders from the British, colonial, French and American Indian perspectives. My book builds on the current interest in the "forgotten theatre" of the Seven Years' War in America by focusing on North Carolina's military role during the struggle.

Finally, it should be noted that my study is a military history of the war, primarily from the perspective of the colony of North Carolina. Those interested in other aspects of this period, such as economic, political or social history, will find fine studies of these fields, a number of which I have listed in the bibliography.

1

THE WAR BEGINS

The hostilities between Great Britain and France in America during the 1750s and early 1760s were part of a long history of conflicts between these two kingdoms dating back to the late seventeenth century and were rooted in European politics and expansion. The first of these conflicts to spill over into North America was the War of the League of Augsburg, known in the colonies as King William's War. This minor struggle erupted in 1688, shortly after William of Orange and his wife, Mary, became England's new Protestant monarchs once the Catholic James II was deposed. France's power under Louis XIV during these years alarmed England, as did its fervent Catholicism and domination of Europe.

The English government also worried about French possession of territory in North America, especially as France's lucrative fur trade posts on the Mississippi River and in the Illinois country increased and the French claimed all the land in the interior wilderness for themselves. France also posed a growing threat to England's seaboard colonies by establishing and strengthening a string of forts, outposts and villages from Quebec on the St. Lawrence River to the Gulf of Mexico. During King William's War, Americans in the northern colonies suffered French and Indian attacks on the frontiers, while English troops failed to take both Montreal and Quebec in 1690. The conflict in America ended in 1697, with neither side gaining any real advantage.

War flared up again in 1702 in Europe during the War of the Spanish Succession, a conflict over who would become the king of Spain after the death of Charles II in 1700. This conflict, known as Queen Anne's War in the American colonies, was fought primarily along the border between the French and English colonies in the North, the scene of numerous raids and massacres and the destruction of towns and farms. The fighting resulted in the capture of Newfoundland and Acadia by English forces before the war's end in 1713. The English colonies also battled Spain (France's ally) in Florida, although the fighting in the South was indecisive.

Over two decades later, the War of the Austrian Succession (1740–1748) involved most of Europe in a group of conflicts over territorial and dynastic disputes following the death of the Holy Roman Emperor Charles VI. The British feared French supremacy in Europe and territorial gains in America and the islands of the West Indies. By 1744, the war became primarily a fight between France and Britain, although the Prussians under Frederick the Great were actively involved against their bitter Austrian enemies as well.

In America, this military contest was called King George's War, after the British monarch on the throne at the time, George II, who reigned from 1727 to 1760. During this conflict, British military officials launched a joint land and sea expedition in 1741 against the fortified Spanish port of Cartagena in modern Colombia. The ambitious campaign included the embodiment of a large regiment of 3,373 officers and men raised in the American colonies. The expedition, an unqualified disaster for the British and colonial force, included hundreds of North Carolina soldiers, few of whom ever returned from the Caribbean theater. This war also impacted North Carolinians in September 1748, when two Spanish ships sailed up the Cape Fear River and attacked the port town of Brunswick. A small force of armed locals drove off an enemy landing party a few days later but only after citizens lost £1,000 in property and suffered several casualties.

On a brighter note, a force of New England colonists supported by British navy warships managed to capture the French fortress at Louisbourg on Cape Breton Island in 1745, although once the war ended in 1748, British diplomats returned this strategic bastion to the French as part of the peace settlement. The duration of the conflict and its financial drain eventually led the weary European powers to negotiate a truce, the Treaty of Aix-la-Chapelle. Signed in 1748, this treaty was more of an armistice or cease-fire in Europe, not a true end to the conflict, especially in the Americas.

The final colonial struggle between Britain and France for supremacy in North America was what Americans have come to call the French and Indian War (1754–1763), part of a global conflict now known as the Seven Years' War or "the Great War for Empire." Many of the old antagonisms between

European powers had remained since the previous war, especially between France and Great Britain in the New World. As one recent historian has noted, "The Seven Years' War was…essentially a continuation of the War of the Austrian Succession," since Britain and France continued to skirmish in their colonies, on the high seas and in India.[3] The Seven Years' War quickly became a worldwide struggle, involving by 1756 France, Britain, Russia, Austria and Prussia after the initial hostilities began in the frontier wilderness of America two years earlier.

Something of a "cold war" existed after the 1748 Treaty of Aix-la-Chapelle between the French in Canada and the valleys of the Mississippi and Ohio Rivers and the British colonies along the Atlantic seaboard. Both of the former belligerents sought to lure North American Indian tribes into their commercial and military spheres of influence—or at least keep them neutral. In search of trade opportunities, small numbers of British entrepreneurs began to move across the Appalachian Mountains toward the upper Ohio River Valley, while land company investors and speculators sought to obtain huge property grants to resell to future settlers. Pennsylvania and Virginia commercial interests also tried to muscle into the fur trade by establishing posts west of the Appalachians, which had long been the purview of French traders.

The colonial French government, headquartered in Quebec, sought to block these alarming English encroachments into what it considered to be its own territory, by right of earlier exploration and occupation. It feared that determined American colonists would eventually settle the fertile Ohio Country, which would block communications from New France (Canada) to the French settlements along the Mississippi River and in the Louisiana and Illinois Territories, including New Orleans. It began to construct new forts in this vast, sparsely settled wilderness to protect its scattered possessions, including the upper reaches of the Ohio River, where daring Pennsylvania, Maryland and Virginia traders and surveyors were already intruding.

As part of their new defensive measures, in 1753, French officials sent a strong force to construct a chain of earth-and-log forts to link Lake Erie with the strategic point called the Forks of the Ohio. This was the confluence of the Allegheny and the Monongahela Rivers, which combined to form the Ohio River at today's city of Pittsburgh. When French colonial troops arrived at the Forks in April 1754, they found a small contingent of Virginia provincial soldiers already building a stockade fort there, in what the French regarded as their own domain. Virginians had also established trading

The British North American colonies and New France during the French and Indian War. *George Park Fisher*, The Colonial Era, *1896.*

storehouses opposite the mouth of Wills Creek on the Potomac River, which also displeased the French.

The French soldiers constructed Fort Duquesne—a square earth-and-log fort with four bastions, outer works and a palisade to the east—after forcing the outnumbered Virginians to leave the Forks. This stronghold and three smaller forts between the Forks and Lake Erie would effectively block American commercial enterprises west of the mountains if they were allowed to stand by colonial leaders. A combination of powerful Virginian and British investors, along with imperial authorities bent on defeating the French in the American wilderness, moved to evict the French from this remote area with military force in the spring of 1754—the first of three such endeavors launched against Fort Duquesne during the war.

British authorities in London reacted promptly once apprised of the French military threats on the west side of the Appalachian Mountains. The secretary of state for the Southern Department (responsible for the British Crown's American colonies) Robert Darcy, the earl of Holderness, sent a letter in August 1753 to all American colonial governors warning them of the French danger to the west and that they should force the French off British territory by peaceful means if possible. The colonies were permitted to raise troops to meet "Force by Force," in the words of the secretary, if the French could not be made to withdraw quietly. With few British soldiers stationed in America at the time, this would mean military action by the colonies themselves.[4]

This set of instructions stirred Virginia's lieutenant governor Robert Dinwiddie into action by the beginning of 1754. He saw the immediate need for a military response to France's aggressive program of fort construction in the Ohio region, as well as its influence among the Indians there. Governor Dinwiddie ordered the deployment of a regiment of Virginia provincial

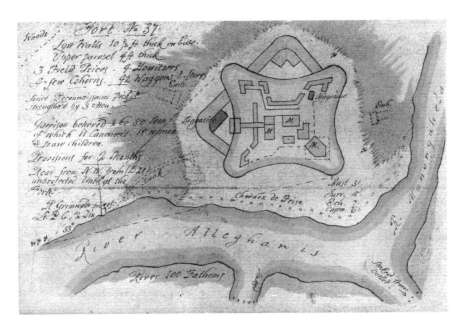

Fort Duquesne, built by the French in 1754 in western Pennsylvania to control the Ohio River Valley. *The Historical Society of Pennsylvania.*

soldiers to the western frontier, commanded by a young, ambitious militia officer named George Washington. Lieutenant Colonel Washington had planned to supervise construction of the Virginia fort at the Forks. When his men were prevented from doing so by the French in April, he instead strengthened the stockade built by Maryland provincial troops on a hill on the north bank of the Potomac River at Wills Creek. He named it Fort Cumberland, which today is the city of Cumberland, Maryland.

About seventy miles southeast of the Forks of the Ohio, Washington built at the Great Meadows a circular log palisade, which he named Fort Necessity. He garrisoned this hastily constructed post with provincial troops recruited for frontier duty, the Virginia Regiment. It was joined by an independent company of British regulars from South Carolina. Washington and Dinwiddie hoped to receive reinforcements and additional supplies from other American colonies in their efforts to control the strategic river junction and defend the backcountry from hostile Indians and French troops.

In January 1754, Dinwiddie sent a circular letter to his fellow colonial governors in Pennsylvania, Massachusetts, New York, New Jersey, Maryland, North Carolina and South Carolina, asking for soldiers, supplies and money "to defeat the designs of the French."[5] Virginia's hopes for intercolonial cooperation went largely unfulfilled, however, as only North Carolina responded to Virginia's plea for assistance. By the 1750s, the various North American colonies were not a united collection of governments bound by mutual interests. Most of the colonies were rivals with one another in terms of trade, culture, religion and land acquisition, and many were more closely aligned to Great Britain than to their fellow American provinces. An attempt to create a cooperative union of the colonies at a meeting of their representatives in Albany, New York in 1754 failed in the face of opposition, mistrust or disinterest. Thus, when Dinwiddie called on other colonies to assist Virginia's efforts to expel the French from the Ohio Valley, most were disinclined to help in what they saw as Virginia's attempt to obtain valuable lands and lucrative trade for its own commercial interests, not for the good of the British Empire.

Given North Carolina's weak political and economic situation in the prewar years, the colony's contribution to Virginia's military enterprise is surprising. Up to the French and Indian War (and long after it), North Carolina had a well-deserved reputation as a poor, contentious and politically divided colony. With few good harbors for large ocean-going ships, the province was economically limited and dependent on Virginia and South Carolina for access to commercial markets. North Carolina had also seen several internal rebellions and devastating Indian wars over the previous decades. Internal political divisions often prevented effective government. Factions developed over the years that created conflicts between the eastern counties and the backcountry and between Albemarle Sound planters and their Cape Fear counterparts. The backcountry was also known as a lawless region populated by people of questionable character, loose morals and little interest in being taxed, governed or recruited for military duty.[6]

Despite this history, Nathaniel Rice, president of North Carolina's colonial council (the governor's appointed advisors) after the death of Governor Gabriel Johnston in 1752, noted that "the Country enjoys great quietness, and is in a flourishing condition, the western parts settling very fast, & much shipping frequenting our rivers."[7] Another observer, however, saw the colony on the eve of war differently. Moravian religious leader August Gottlieb Spangenberg wrote that some of the colonists were "naturally indolent and sluggish. Others have come here from England, Scotland, & from the Northern Colonies[,] some have settled here on account of poverty as they wished to own land & were too poor to buy in Pennsylvania or New Jersey." The minister also reported that other Carolinians were "refugees from justice or have fled from debt; or have left a wife & children elsewhere,—or possibly to escape the penalty of some other crime; under the impression that they could remain here unmolested & with impunity." He also saw that "bands of horse thieves have been infesting portions of the State & pursuing their nefarious calling a long time," which was "the reason North Carolina has such an unenviable reputation among the neighbouring provinces."[8]

Upon the death of council president Rice in January 1753, Matthew Rowan of Brunswick County became president of the council (in effect, acting governor until one could be appointed by King George II). He and other Carolina officials began to prepare for the possibility of war with France in the American wilderness, given the news of French activities on the Ohio River and warnings from London. In late May, the North Carolina Assembly (the colony's legislative body, often called the "lower house") enacted a law to erect a fortification on the Outer Banks at Ocracoke Inlet, between Core Banks and Ocracoke Island, to prevent French maritime raids on the colony's coastal port towns.[9] Rowan and his council also tried to refurbish the colony's militia organization, which in the preceding years "had been very much neglected." He was pleased to report in particular that in the far western frontier counties of Anson, Orange and Rowan, "there is now at least three thousand [men,] for the most part Irish Protestants and Germans and dayley increasing" available for militia service.[10]

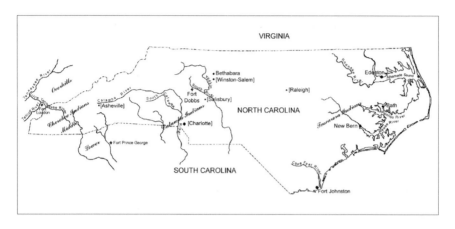

North Carolina during the French and Indian War (western border is modern). *Map from Maass, "All This Poor Province Could Do."*

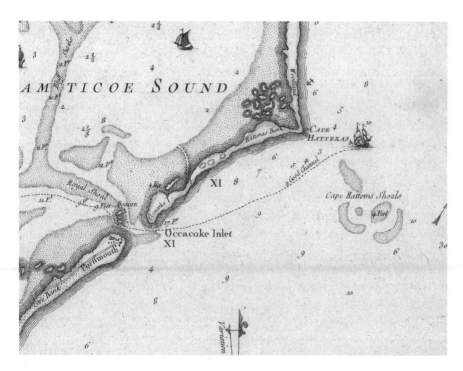

Detail of postwar map showing Ocracoke and the new town of Portsmouth, fortified during the war. *North Carolina Collection, Wilson Library, UNC–Chapel Hill.*

Fortunately for Carolina officials, for their western defense, they could rely in part on the Catawba Indians (or Nation), who at the time of the French and Indian War were living along the border of North and South Carolina, along the Catawba River south of modern Charlotte. In the first half of the eighteenth century, this native group absorbed the remnants of several other Indian peoples devastated by warfare with European settlers and other indigenous tribes. Moreover, the Catawba Nation suffered from disease epidemics over the years, particularly a 1738 smallpox outbreak, which may have killed as much as half of the populace. Warriors from northern tribes occasionally attacked Catawba villages and limited their trade, while drought and famine in the early 1750s added to their distress. Records show that in 1756, the North Carolina Governor's Council allotted fifty pounds to "buy corn for the use of the Catawba Indians," who were "in great want of corn at this time and subsist by begging from the neighbouring Planters and thereby obliged to Quit their families and oppress the Planters who are themselves scarce of Corn yet Dare not Deny them."[11] During the conflict with France, the Catawbas sided with the British and provided frontier patrols, guides and auxiliaries to colonial and red-coated forces throughout the struggle, with an initial strength of about three hundred warriors.[12]

Although the colony's frontier was not under widespread attack in 1754, that summer, several Catawba Indians killed two Frenchmen and three of their Indian allies, evidently part of a scouting party, in a skirmish only two miles from the Rowan County courthouse. Matthew Rowan planned to "order the Militia to be in redyness" on the frontier and boasted that he would "not suffer any insult or incrochment on his Majesty's Dominions in This Province whilst the administration is in my hands."[13] The British government's Board of Trade, the official committee responsible for matters involving the colonies, responded positively to Rowan at the end of the year that his "endeavours to put the Militia upon a better foot show a proper regard and attention to the interest and security of the colony." The possibility of actual war was becoming more evident.[14]

Rowan also received a letter that fall from Southern Department secretary Holderness warning of potential French and Indian attacks. The secretary directed him to be on guard and to promote North Carolina's military cooperation with other American provinces for mutual defense. Likewise, in July 1754, Thomas Robinson, Holderness's successor as Southern Department secretary, wrote to Rowan, advising him that "it is His Majty's express Command, that You should, in obedience thereto, not only act vigorously in the Defence of the Government under your Care, but that

You should likewise be aiding and assisting His Majesty's other American Colonies, to repel any hostile Attempts made against Them." These requests for defensive measures and colonial cooperation, however, came after North Carolina had already decided to come to Virginia's aid.[15]

Back in February 1754, Rowan had received Dinwiddie's appeal for aid "to dispossess the French of a settlement they have made at the Ohio within the undoubted limits of Virginia." Rowan worried that if the French established themselves on the upper Ohio, "they will secure the Gaps of the mountains and destroy our settlements at their Pleasure," presumably with their Indian allies pouring into the Carolina backcountry and destroying communities there. He summoned the assembly to meet at New Bern. By the end of the legislative session in March, the assembly voted to issue £12,000 in paper money "for raising and providing for a regiment of 750 effective men to be sent to the Assistance of Virginia," £2,000 to repair and complete Fort Johnston at the mouth of the Cape Fear River and £2,000 to complete the unfinished fort at Ocracoke Inlet. It also approved of spending "£1,000 to buy arms and ammunition for the poorer Inhabitants of Rowan & Anson Countys being most exposed" to potential Indian attacks in the backcountry. London officials frowned on colonies' issuing their own paper currency due to its questionable commercial value, but in this case, it was North Carolina's only way of raising funds for military preparations. Hard currency and credit were always scarce within its borders.[16]

Governor Dinwiddie was pleased at the news that his southern neighbor would assist Virginia's efforts to thwart the French and prevent them from erecting new forts. "Every Gov't except No. Caro. has amus'd me with Expectations that have proved fruitless," he wrote, "and at length refuse to give any Supply."[17] He had earlier written to Matthew Rowan that "it gives me much Pleasure to observe the Loyalty and Readiness of your Assembly in raising Money for the Good of the Common Cause." Upon learning that North Carolina would also raise a large regiment of provincial soldiers, Dinwiddie was appreciative, but he informed Rowan that North Carolina would have to pay and supply its own troops while in service, "as it is for the general Safety of the Whole." He also complained that North Carolina recruits would be paid higher wages than his Virginia soldiers, which could create jealousies and dissent within their ranks.[18]

The North Carolina Regiment embodied in 1754 was not a militia organization. Rather, it was a military force raised specifically for service in Virginia (and elsewhere) for a specific duration during this imperial crisis. It was commanded by Colonel James Innes, a man of "Capacity, Judgment

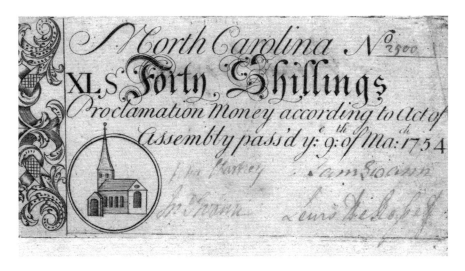

North Carolina paper currency issued by the assembly in March 1754 to fund the colony's grant of aid to the British war efforts. *Colonial Williamsburg Foundation, Museum Purchase.*

and cool Conduct," in Dinwiddie's assessment. Likewise, one of Innes's acquaintances wrote (in 1755) that "every Body in this province (one only excepted) readily acknowledges Colonel Innes's fitness for the Task he is engaged in." The Scottish-born Innes had moved to North Carolina in 1733, probably with prior military experience. After settling on the Northeast Cape Fear River at Point Pleasant plantation, Innes led one of North Carolina's four companies in the ill-fated Cartagena expedition in 1740, part of the War of Jenkin's Ear against Spain. In this campaign in the tropics, most of North Carolina's four hundred troops perished of disease and malnutrition, and few saw any actual fighting. Only twenty-five of Innes's company of one hundred soldiers returned to their Cape Fear homes after the campaign.[19] Innes also began serving on the Governor's Council in 1750 and remained in that role until his death in 1759, having earned a sterling reputation within the colony.

Virginia's governor recommended in March 1754 that the Carolina troops come by sea to the port town of Alexandria on the Potomac River, rather than marching overland, in order to quicken their progress.[20] That month, Innes informed Dinwiddie that he would soon bring his force of 750 men, although he complained of his age and ill health while mobilizing the troops.[21] Innes visited Virginia in April, and Dinwiddie—a fellow Scot—was "very much pleas'd with [the North Carolina Assembly's] readiness in granting Supplies on this emergent Occasion."[22]

In June, the British Crown appointed Innes "to be Com'd'r in Chief of all the Forces already rais'd and destin'd, or that shall hereafter be rais'd, design'd and ordered on the Service of the said Expedit'n" to repel the French on the Ohio River. This was surely an indication of his high qualifications.[23] Innes's martial reputation prompted Colonel Washington to "rejoice that I am likely to be happy under the command of an experienced Officer and man of Sense."[24]

Colonel Innes faced significant challenges trying to embody his new command. Although the legislature authorized a regiment of 750 recruits for Virginia's assistance, by June, it had become obvious that if North Carolina was expected to supply and feed its men when serving in Virginia or on the Ohio River, there would be formidable difficulties doing so. Matthew Rowan informed London officials that "we have but very little silver and gold here," which "has laid us under great difficultys" procuring supplies and equipping the recruits. Moreover, the colony lacked arms to issue to the new troops. Due to the heavy expense of keeping the men in service, the colony reduced the size of the regiment to 450 soldiers in four companies, some of which Innes planned to send to Alexandria by water at "the first fair wind," while the rest would begin their march in early June.[25]

While Innes struggled to get his regiment in order, Rowan tried to revitalize the colony's militia, which had "fallen much to decay." Each of the province's twenty-two counties began to form a regiment of foot, while Rowan worked to raise seventeen troops of dragoons, which would be "of great service in case of any sudden attack." He estimated the size of the colony's militia at fifteen thousand men, and he had about four hundred dragoons in service by the summer, though somewhat unevenly armed and equipped.[26]

As Carolinians prepared for war, events in the backcountry of Pennsylvania, Maryland and Virginia turned out disastrously for Colonel Washington and his forces. Washington surprised and defeated a small French party in a skirmish in May 1754 and then concentrated his soldiers at Great Meadows, where his men had built Fort Necessity. Here, his command was attacked by French and Indian forces on July 3 and had to surrender the following day. The French permitted Washington to withdraw his men to Fort Cumberland and then destroyed Fort Necessity and most of the Virginians' baggage and supplies before withdrawing west to Fort Duquesne.

While the Virginians fought the French and Indians in Pennsylvania, Colonel Innes struggled to get the reduced North Carolina Regiment to the scene of action. The regiment's first objective was the small Shenandoah Valley town

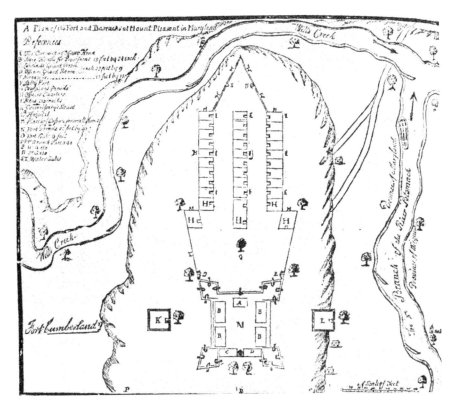

Fort Cumberland, at the mouth of Wills Creek on the Potomac River in western Maryland. *William Lowdermilk*, History of Cumberland, (Maryland), *1878*.

of Winchester, Virginia, from where they would march to Fort Cumberland. Unfortunately, Innes's troops were plagued with delays and obstacles on their journey and were unable to support Washington's operations that summer. Three of the North Carolina companies, under captains Rowan, McKilware and Vail, reached Alexandria at the end of June by ship. Innes and his 150 soldiers marched to Leesburg within a few days and then through the Blue Ridge at Vestal's Gap to Winchester. The troops arrived there on July 9— five days after Washington had surrendered Fort Necessity. These Carolinians "were for want of a Magazine in N Carolina unarmed," and no weapons had been sent from Williamsburg for their use. Fortunately, Maryland's governor Horatio Sharpe, upon Innes's "earnest Request...sent immediately to Winchester 150 Stand of Arms for the use of the Companies under his Command."[27]

The Potomac River near Alexandria, Virginia. Carolina troops traveled on these waters three times during the war en route to western Pennsylvania and Maryland. *Author photo.*

Dinwiddie complained to Colonel Innes that the North Carolina companies were to blame for Washington's defeat at Fort Necessity, "owing to the delay of Your Forces." The Virginia executive reported that the Carolina troops' money had been squandered to the point that the company officers called on him to pay the troops out of Virginia funds. The Carolinians had driven a herd of hogs along with them for food and to sell in Virginia for the soldiers' pay, but Dinwiddie reported that "the Pork gives but a poor Prospect of rais'g Money from its Condition…You can have no dependence on it for Cash, unless You order it to be sold at public Vendue." Dinwiddie reluctantly advanced funds to the Carolina companies as North Carolina currency was not accepted in Virginia due to its dubious reputation in other colonies.[28]

Continuing to blame North Carolina in a letter to Sharpe, Dinwiddie claimed that Washington's defeat and the surrender of Fort Necessity was due in part to "the N. Carolina Forces disbanding themselves; which was occasioned by a monstrous mismanagement of them from the Beginning." Virginia's executive held that the Carolina soldiers were paid too much, "so that their Money was wholly expended before they joined the other Forces," and the men refused to serve in Virginia at a lower pay rate. Innes's regiment was paid three shillings a day, whereas the Virginia men only received 8 pence per diem. He also concluded that the high rate of pay for the "elated" Carolina soldiers made for "slow marches." "This is monstrous ill Conduct," Dinwiddie fumed.[29]

In a letter to Baron Grantham in September 1754, Dinwiddie spelled out his complaint against North Carolina's regiment in greater detail. Matthew Rowan "gave the private Men, 3 [shillings] per Day, and the officers near the same." Unfortunately, "the Dillatoriness of their Forces marching, with the excessive high Pay to the Private Men, exhausted the £12,000, before they had properly joined the other Forces." Then, the Carolina troops balked at further service "without Assurances of the Continuance of said Pay…which by no means could be complied with, as the other Men had only 8d. Per Day; at [that] Pay they would not serve, so deserted in large Parties."[30]

Dinwiddie's criticism was not without merit. Lacking money, provisions and supplies, Innes had considered disbanding his regiment even before it reached Winchester, although Dinwiddie urged him to keep them embodied. They did not impress South Carolina governor James Glenn. Innes's troops were "neither disciplined nor armed," he reported, and "what few arms they had were of different calibers—some wide bores, some small bores; but a great part of them had no arms at all." Without muskets available to issue to the troops in the colony, the regiment's officers were burdened with finding all manner of powder, shot and bullet moulds for the troops.[31]

While the poor service of Innes's regiment was indeed embarrassing and these soldiers would have added strength to British colonial power on the frontier, Dinwiddie's assignment of blame to the Carolinians was misdirected. He could have pointed to those colonies that sent no troops to Virginia's aid as well. George Washington's inept performance that ultimately led to the surrender of Fort Necessity was also to blame. Still Dinwiddie pinned the culpability on Innes's troops: the "unexpected Desert'n of so many [North Carolina] Men has entirely put an End to the Operat's I had intended this Fall," Virginia's executive concluded.[32]

In addition to other command challenges, Innes also faced an uprising among his troops late in July. The fourth company of the North Carolina Regiment, presumably raised in the western counties, marched by land under Captain Bryan northward into Virginia's Shenandoah Valley on the Great Wagon Road and was at Augusta Courthouse (now Staunton) by July 27. At this small frontier hamlet, Dinwiddie reported, the company "mutinied, and would go no further without Money." A friend of the Virginia governor lent Captain Bryan forty pounds "to quiet their Mutiny," but even after this attempt to mollify the rebellious soldiers, they seem to have returned to North Carolina without proceeding farther north.[33]

As of early August, none of Innes's soldiers had reached Fort Cumberland. Dinwiddie tried to help the Carolinians and sent Innes "Small Arms, Bayonets, Powder, and Shott" for his troops, but otherwise reiterated to Innes that Virginia "will maintain none but their own Forces."[34] Likewise, council president Matthew Rowan reported to London officials in late August that "we have now in Virginia in His Majesty's service near four hundred men under the command of very good Officers which we subsist[,] but our Fund will not last above three months longer at which time they must return if not subsisted by his Majesty or some of the Provinces that have not furnished men."[35] Eventually, Governor Dinwiddie recognized that the Carolina regiment was more trouble that it was worth: "I now wish that we had none from your colony but yourself," he wrote to Colonel Innes, "for I foresee nothing but confusion among them."[36]

Colonel Innes reluctantly disbanded the troubled North Carolina Regiment at Winchester on August 11, "for want of subsistence," although the colony had sent a herd of beef cattle to Winchester by that time. Rowan complained to London that "a very small sum with good words would have kept them together."[37] Innes attempted to entice enough men to remain with him to form one company, and it appears that forty to fifty Carolinians remained embodied at Fort Cumberland as late as September. Many of these men enlisted in the Maryland forces upon being discharged by Colonel Innes,[38] and at least one man enlisted in a British independent company, but he later deserted.[39]

North Carolina's efforts to participate in Britain's undeclared war against the French and their Indian allies began with enthusiasm, a large regiment of provincial soldiers and a significant fund for supporting the troops and building forts. The disintegration of the regiment and financial difficulties showed the colony that waging war in America was a difficult and expensive undertaking. Soon, however, the colony would have a new governor in place to coordinate future military measures, perhaps with greater success than was realized in 1754.

2

THE COLONY FIGHTS AN IMPERIAL WAR

B y the early autumn of 1754, Matthew Rowan and many of his fellow Carolinians were eagerly awaiting the arrival of North Carolina's new colonial governor, sixty-five-year-old Arthur Dobbs, who had been appointed captain general and governor in chief of North Carolina in January 1753 by King George II. Born in Scotland and raised at Carrickfergus Castle in County Antrim, Ireland, he had purchased land in western North Carolina years before he arrived in America and had enthusiastically encouraged Irish Protestants to settle there. He was also a passionate imperialist, with a touchy sense of the king's rights—the "royal prerogative"—when dealing with provincials in his new home. After first landing in Virginia, Dobbs arrived in North Carolina at the end of October 1754 and lived at Brunswick, on the lower Cape Fear River.

The new governor wasted little time preparing his colony for war, even before he arrived in America. In England, he petitioned the king in April 1753 for military assistance for North Carolina, specifically for "Ordnance and Stores necessary" for Fort Johnston "for the safety of the Colony and shipping."[40] Before he crossed the Atlantic, Dobbs also arranged to have one thousand Dutch-made flintlock muskets and accouterments—cartridge boxes, belts, frogs and bayonets—shipped from England to North Carolina for use in the colony.

Soon after Dobbs's arrival, he requested from each county militia commander "an exact list of the men in their several districts capable of bearing arms, with an account how they were armed & what ammunition

Ruins of St. Philip's Anglican Church at Brunswick, North Carolina on the Cape Fear River. Governor Arthur Dobbs took up residence in the town and is buried in the church's graveyard. *Brunswick Town/Fort Anderson State Historic Site.*

they had." He found little gunpowder in the colony, and few serviceable arms, "and those given to me by His Majesty are not yet arrived from Virginia." Unable to act until the next session of the assembly, Dobbs could do little until then. He asked the Board of Trade to send to North Carolina "twenty or thirty barrells [*sic*] of Powder and a proportionable quantity of Balls; which if not otherwise to be had, shall be repaid out of the Powder duty which I expect will be raised by Act of Assembly; since at present we have no credit and must pay double price, if any is imported by merchants." He also suggested that in light of the expected violence on the western frontier, "it will be necessary to erect a Fort beyond our farthest settlers to protect that Frontier and our Indian Allies...I hope therefore your Lordships will represent to His Majesty the necessity there is of having a Company of 100 men established here for these purposes."[41]

Dobbs also reported on the condition of Fort Johnston on the Cape Fear River, guarding the towns of Wilmington and Brunswick upstream. This fort, authorized by the assembly in 1745 but not started until 1748, had a garrison as early as 1751. It was "very small, but large enough to Defend the Lower Battery," which was situated to "Command the Ships which go up or

North Carolina governor Arthur Dobbs, an ardent supporter of British war efforts during his twelve-year term. *Colonial Williamsburg Foundation, Museum Purchase.*

come down the River," once the proper ordnance was in place. At the end of 1754, the fort's rampart and parapet were "faced only with Strong Pine Trees Cut into large Planks 6 inches thick, Sloping inwards, to support the Rampart, and the parapet which is railed no higher than the guns without embrasures." There were only five six-pounder guns and four two-pounders at the fort, salvaged from an old ship. This antiquated ordnance was too light to prevent large enemy ships from passing the fort. Dobbs was amazed that the fort had "no garrison but 2 or 3 men to keep the fort and this was all the safety in the Province to defend the most navigable river in the Province." The governor also noted that a fort or battery at Topsail Inlet near Beaufort "to protect our ships in time of war as to prevent Privateers from Sheltering there and Interrupting our Ships" was also underway.[42]

In late December, once the new governor made an initial assessment of the military situation in the colony, he began to recognize the difficulties North Carolina faced in supporting the war. There was little hard money in the colony, and its paper currency was not accepted beyond its borders. Dobbs had to find funds to finish the "fortifications at Ocracoke and Core Sound, [and] to pay the troops we shall be able to raise." The governor was eager to put three hundred soldiers in independent companies in the field, recruited to serve as disciplined British regulars. The assembly, however, never allowed the funds for this kind of professional troops.[43]

Nevertheless, Dobbs labored to get North Carolina to provide as much money and as many men as it could muster to defeat the French. He dramatically advised the colony's council in December 1754 that "the fire which has caught your Neighbours house has lately spread into your own, your religion Liberty and property are all at stake if [not] repelled & drove back to their Inhospitable Colonies."[44] Dobbs also hoped they would recognize "the Necessity there is of granting a reasonable and immediate supply [for the war] and entering into a plan of union with all the British Colonies for our mutual future defence."[45]

North Carolina's government began to hear reports of Indian attacks in the western backcountry in the fall of 1754. Militia officer John Clark, for example, reported from the area along the Broad River near the border of North and South Carolina that sixteen people had been killed and ten were missing, "which we suppose to be killed or carried away captive." Clark did not think the Indians who committed the murders were French influenced, but he did ask for "support of our back settlements." The settlers needed "men with arms & ammunition sufficient to range the frontiers of our settlements to keep the enemy off us." Dobbs received other reports of frontier violence as well, once he arrived in the province, and sent what little powder he could procure to the back counties.[46]

Dobbs also collected information about the colony's militia forces in 1754 from reports by county military officers. The reports he received were not encouraging. In Beaufort County, for example, there were "no arms in the publick store," as was also the case in Carteret, Chowan, Duplin, Onslow and several other counties. Bertie County had no officers for its regiment, while in Bladen County the "fines [were] not high enough to oblige the Militia to attend musters." Most western counties did not even respond to Dobbs's request for returns.[47]

The colony's assembly met in December 1754 at New Bern and voted to print £8,000 of paper money for the war effort, "to be employed in the Assistance of Virginia & Defence of this Frontier." The representatives also allowed for 100 men for two years of service in one company and a second company of 50 men "for the Defence of this frontier, having had so many lately murder'd by the French Indians, and French in the Indian Dress," according to Dobbs. This was a significantly lower number of troops than the 750 men the previous assembly had raised to help Virginia, but the disintegration of Innes's regiment must have taught the legislators a painful lesson. The governor reported that the colony could do no more on account of "the ill state of the Revenue here...there being neither Bullion nor Coin in the Country, by which the Troops can be paid when they go out of the province."[48]

Dobbs also hoped to erect a new fort at Cape Lookout, on the Outer Banks, to protect "our Merchants & small Cruisers, as to prevent our Enemies from lying there in safety," although no money was available from the colony to build it. Dobbs once again asked the Board of Trade to provide an independent company of one hundred soldiers on the British establishment, "to garrison these forts and one on our Frontier."[49]

The raising of men and money by the North Carolina Assembly at the end of 1754 was only a small part of the overall efforts of the British government to prepare for the coming conflict, although war had yet to be declared officially against France. For 1755, officials in London decided to raise more troops in the colonies for offensives against the French in the Ohio Valley, at Fort Niagara on Lake Ontario, at Fort St. Frederic on Lake Champlain and in Nova Scotia, under the overall leadership of a single British commander in America. To lead these operations, the Crown assigned sixty-year-old Major General Edward Braddock of the Coldstream Guards, who would bring with him two incomplete battalions of British regulars—the Forty-fourth and Forty-eighth Regiments—from Ireland to Virginia as part of the expedition to capture Fort Duquesne. The march to the Ohio was to be led personally by Braddock, who arrived in Virginia in February 1755. Imperial authorities—especially Braddock—

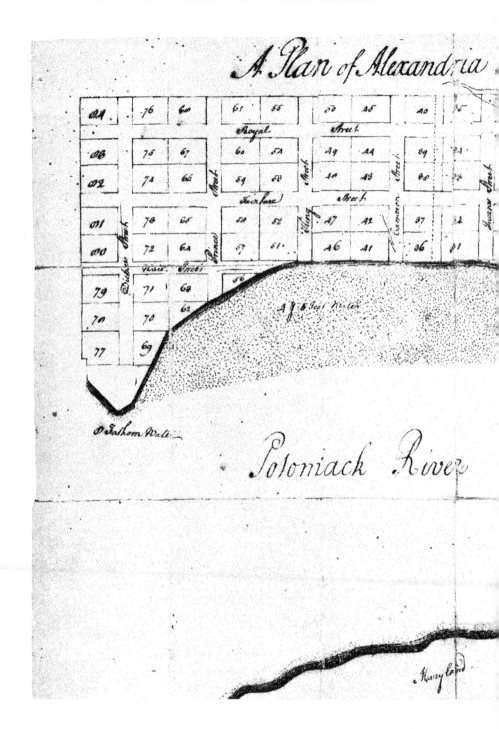

"A Plan of Alexandria," by George Washington. North Carolina troops debarked at the small Potomac River town on their way to join British forces on campaign in 1754, 1755 and 1758. *From* History of the George Washington Bicentennial Celebration, *vol. 1.*

Braddock's route from Fort Cumberland to his army's defeat near Fort Duquesne. Captain Edward Dobbs's company of Carolinians went as far as Dunbar's Camp. *From* History of the George Washington Bicentennial Celebration, *vol. 1.*

expected each colony to support these campaigns vigorously and to add recruits to the two regiments the general brought with him. The soldiers authorized by the North Carolina Assembly were to be organized into companies and then sent to join Braddock's army at Alexandria, where the troops for the Ohio campaign would be gathered.[50]

Braddock planned to march his force of regulars and provincial troops from Alexandria to Winchester and then through the Allegheny Mountains to Fort Cumberland on the Potomac. From there, the British column would have to construct its own road through a dense wilderness over creeks, marshes, rivers and high mountains to the Forks of the Ohio, in order to attack and capture Fort Duquesne. The new road would have to accommodate Braddock's numerous wagons and artillery and be capable of supporting logistics for the troops, as there would be nowhere to obtain adequate supplies for the large army once it left Fort Cumberland. It was a daunting task, for which Braddock and most of his officers were ill-prepared and which the American colonies were reluctant to support.

North Carolina's company of one hundred men served in Braddock's expedition under the command of Captain Edward Brice Dobbs, the twenty-eight-year-old son of the governor and holder of a lieutenant's commission in the Royal Fusiliers. At least some of these new soldiers were clothed in blue wool regimental coats with red cuffs and facings, along with blue breeches, which most of the troops received in Alexandria from Virginia's military stores. Some of the soldiers carried .78-caliber to .80-caliber Dutch muskets made in the 1730s, sent over to the colony by British officials in London at the new governor's request. Others may have shouldered British muskets of large caliber (usually .76 caliber to .78 caliber) or whatever firelocks could be procured within the colony or in Virginia. Each man also received a belt, bayonet, scabbard, frog and belly box for his cartridges, which together made up a stand of arms commonly issued to provincials and militiamen when on campaign.[51] In addition to the soldiers, Captain Dobbs's men included teamsters, among them a young man from the Carolina backcountry near the Yadkin River, Daniel Boone.[52]

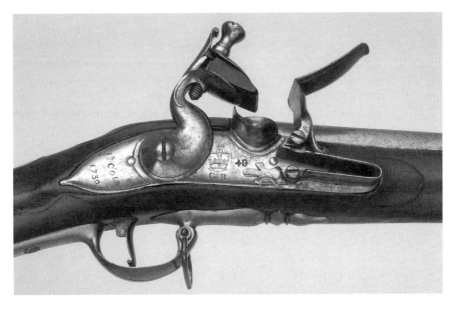

Lock detail of an original British .75-caliber Long Land Pattern flintlock musket, commonly issued to colonial troops during the French and Indian War. *Private collection.*

In April 1755, Captain Dobbs's troops sailed from North Carolina into the Chesapeake Bay and then up the Potomac River to Alexandria, which they reached in a few weeks. By this time, Braddock had moved most of his troops to Fort Cumberland, "a small piece of ground inclosed [sic] with a Strong [log] Palisade joined pretty close." Governor Dinwiddie noted that Dobbs's company consisted of eighty-four soldiers, having lost some of the men through desertion and illness since leaving home. After disembarking at the wharfs of Alexandria, Captain Dobbs—"a well behaved young gentleman," according to Dinwiddie—led his command westward a few days later by way of Leesburg to Winchester. The Carolinians went on from there to arrive at Fort Cumberland by late May, at which time, the company was reduced to only seventy-two soldiers. Prior to marching overland for the frontier, Dinwiddie had to provide Dobbs's poorly equipped company with "Powder and Shott" and some uniforms.[53]

Supplying and paying the soldiers was problematic, as was always the case when North Carolina troops served outside the colony, given the lack of hard money available for military use. Captain Dobbs and the company's officers attempted to alleviate the problem "by buying up cattle and pork &c." to send into Virginia to sell there. Poor markets and low demand, however, led Carolina officials to reship the herds to the Caribbean Islands, "and this disappointment occasioning the pay to fall far short of what was necessary, [Governor Dobbs] was obliged upon my own credit with Colonel [John] Hunter [a Virginia commissary, and the paymaster of Braddock's forces] to take up money to pay the Troops."[54]

By the end of May, the North Carolina soldiers had reached Fort Cumberland. Here, they found James Innes, former commander of the North Carolina Regiment, now acting as the fort's governor, "to superintend the commissaries, and to dispatch the convoys." In organizing his command, General Braddock divided his troops into two brigades and assigned Captain Dobbs's company to the brigade of Colonel Thomas Dunbar, a British regular officer commanding the Forty-eighth Regiment. After reaching the fort, two of Dobbs's men—Richard Shelton and Calbib Curry—decided they had endured enough of army life and deserted. Recaptured almost immediately, the two were tried and convicted on June 6 and were sentenced to receive one thousand lashes each. The following day, "five men of the Carolina companies intended to depart after receiving provisions but were apprehended by one of them who informed on the rest." The four thwarted men were court-martialed, and as one

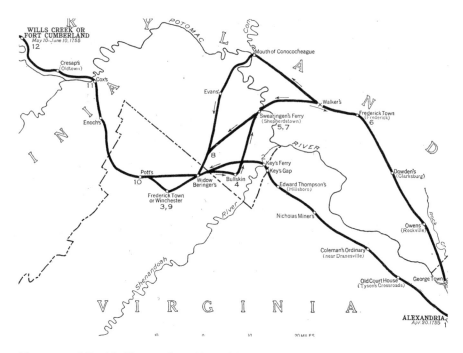

Movement of Braddock's army from Alexandria to Fort Cumberland. North Carolina troops followed the southern route shown on this map. *From* History of the George Washington Bicentennial Celebration, *vol. 1.*

witness reported, "one received a thousand lashes, one nine hundred and the other two, five hundred a piece." What happened to the informant was not reported. Officers learned that these Carolinians intended to desert to the French, far to the west on the Ohio River.[55]

Braddock began his westward advance to Fort Duquesne from Fort Cumberland on June 8, through what he described as "an uninhabited Wilderness over steep rocky mountains and almost impassable Morasses." Dobbs's Carolina company of eighty-one officers and men was in the rear element of the column with Dunbar's redcoats. They left the banks of the Potomac and eventually crossed countless streams and ridges on the rough path hacked out of the woods and mountains. Along with the rest of the army, the North Carolina troops had to traverse Big Savage Mountain and Allegheny Ridge and cross the Savage and Youghiogheny Rivers.[56]

By June 16, the entire army had reached the Little Meadows, only twenty-two miles from Fort Cumberland. Here, after conceding that the expedition's progress suffered delays by the army's excessive baggage train, artillery and the difficult terrain, a frustrated Braddock divided his command into two sections. A strong detachment of troops carrying minimal equipment and few wagons and cannons would march in advance under the general's direct command, constructing a rough trace through the forest as it proceeded. It would be followed by the remainder of the force under Colonel Dunbar and an eight-hundred-man contingent with most of the guns, baggage wagons and stores. The North Carolina company continued under Dunbar's command as they proceeded slowly toward Fort Duquesne.[57]

While Dobbs and his soldiers trudged along the rough trail in the wake of Braddock's advanced detachment, a mixed party of French and Indians set out from Fort Duquesne on July 9 and struck Braddock's advanced column, which had reached a point only a few miles from its objective. The redcoats were taken completely by surprise and were largely untrained in the kind of forest warfare needed to react to the sudden attack. In about three hours of bloody combat, the panicked British lead element was almost completely destroyed. The North Carolinians, far to the rear with Dunbar's brigade, were not involved in the forest bloodbath. They had reached no farther on the road than what is now called Dunbar's Camp, about fifty miles from the scene of Braddock's defeat.

Upon hearing the news of the catastrophe from fleeing soldiers the next day, many of Colonel Dunbar's troops fled in panic, and the camp was thrown into "the greatest confusion." Trying to restore order, Dunbar ordered his men to bury or destroy a large part of the army's stores and artillery, which could not be easily transported back to Wills Creek. This included four cannons, three thousand cannon balls and sixteen thousand pounds of gunpowder. Captain Dobbs's Carolinians retreated with those Dunbar brought under control to Fort Cumberland by July 17. Several days later, Dunbar marched his British regulars to Philadelphia, effectively abandoning the backcountry to enemy attacks from Pennsylvania to the Carolinas. Despite the pleas of colonial officials, Dunbar could not be induced to leave any of his regulars on the frontier.[58]

Once the redcoats abandoned western Maryland, Fort Cumberland's garrison consisted only of provincial troops. In August, Maryland's governor Sharpe reported that "the several Companies that have been raised & supported by the Govts of Virginia[,] N Carolina & Maryland are left to garrison Fort Cumberland & to protect the Frontiers of these Provinces till something farther can be done for their security & for his Majesty's Service."[59] Many Carolinians, however, had seen enough military service so

On July 9, 1755, General Edward Braddock's army met with disaster in the wilderness near the Forks of the Ohio, in which he was mortally wounded. This sketch shows the injured Braddock. *Library of Congress.*

An eighteenth-century swivel gun. *The National Park Service.*

far from home. They began to desert the fort with their arms, stealing horses from the garrison to speed their southward flight. By the end of August, the Fort Cumberland garrison numbered only about 160 troops. Records show that there were just 15 North Carolina provincials at the fort by mid-September and 13 by December.[60]

While Captain Dobbs and his dwindling number of disgruntled soldiers remained at Fort Cumberland, in North Carolina, work continued that summer on the fortifications and battery at Ocracoke, although there was still no artillery to place there. Governor Dobbs reported "an immediate occasion for Artillery and Bullets and Stores" for both Ocracoke and Fort Johnston. At the latter post, he wanted "14 eighteen pounders, and 16 nine pounders, with 30 Swivel [guns] and as many Musquetoons." Gunpowder was always scarce in the colony, so he asked the Board of Trade for twenty barrels of powder and reminded it of the need for cannon and supplies for the two forts.[61]

The governor also worked to "put the frontier in the best State of Defence against the Indian Incursions" by having an additional "100 select men in Readiness to joyn our Frontier Company." The frontier unit, commanded by Captain Hugh Waddell, scouted the backcountry "upon the edges of the mountain," while Dobbs searched the backcountry for a proper place to erect a fort. On a tributary of the south branch of the Yadkin River (near modern Statesville), the governor "found an Eminence and good Springs, and fixed upon that as most central to assist the back settlers and be a retreat to them as it was beyond the well settled Country." Waddell's company would erect barracks for the winter at the spot. Here Dobbs and Waddell met with militia officers of Anson and Rowan Counties, which were exposed on the western frontier. The governor ordered them to choose "fifty men each and a central place of rendezvous to be fixed for each to the northward and Southward of our Frontier Company, to be under Captain Waddell's command, to join him when necessary or for him to march to assist them in case of any incursion."[62]

In Hugh Waddell, Dobbs and the colony had a capable officer, second only in prominence to James Innes among North Carolina's soldiers during the French and Indian War. Born in County Down, Ireland, around 1734, the young officer served as a lieutenant in Innes's regiment in its abortive attempt to support George Washington and the Virginia troops in 1754. During this service, he

Miniature portrait of Colonel Hugh Waddell, prominent officer in the North Carolina forces during the French and Indian War. *Courtesy North Carolina Museum of History.*

was promoted to captain in North Carolina's provincial forces. He had preceded his family's friend Arthur Dobbs to North Carolina, which may explain the young man's appointment the following year as commander of the western soldiers defending the frontier, in newly formed Rowan County. Waddell would receive several promotions and serve actively throughout the war.[63]

While traveling in the western counties in the late summer of 1755, Governor Dobbs learned the shocking news of Braddock's defeat but, soon thereafter, heard from Governor Dinwiddie that his son at Fort Cumberland was not injured, although he did suffer an eye ailment due to exposure to a "stinking weed." Alarmed that the British defeat near Fort Duquesne would open the Carolina frontier settlements to Indian attacks, the governor summoned the provincial council to "meet to consider further of our present Danger" and looked forward to the next meeting of the assembly in late September for additional means with which to "put a speedy End to the French Schemes."[64]

Convening at New Bern, the assembly sent an address to the governor, advising him of its distress at the news of Braddock's defeat, which "has given an unfortunate turn to Affairs in the Neighbouring Provinces." The Indians' "cruelties and Depredations…raises so horrid an Idea of the

bloody Designs of those treacherous people, that it were as impossible…
not to be animated with a proper Resentment at their unparalleled
Outrages." It also pledged to protect the frontier and also to continue
"assistance to the other Governments against the common Enemy."[65]

With these sentiments in mind, it granted £10,000 in paper bills for
aid to the British war effort. The colony also voted to "raise 3 Companies
of 50 Men each to be continued to the first of November 1756," and
£1,000 "to build a Barrack and Fort for the Company on the Western
Frontier," which was later named for the governor. The amount of money
and the number of soldiers were less than the governor had wished for,
but given the precarious state of the colony's finances, little more could
be expected.[66] Dobbs planned to arm the colony's troops with some of the
one thousand stands of arms shipped to North Carolina from Britain, and
some would go to the "Militia of the exposed Counties and near the sea
coast for our Defense."[67] He also tried to gauge the state of the colony's
military preparedness by ordering "a General Muster throughout the
Province," hoping to learn "the Number of the Men in each Company,
with the condition of their Arms and Ammunition."[68]

In addition to imploring the assembly to recruit more men, Dobbs
asked the legislators to address the chronic problem of desertion from
the provincial companies. "From the base Principals in the lowest class of
men for want of education," Dobbs wrote, deserting soldiers often "carry
off their arms and livery and steal horses to carry them away, and appear
publickly in this Province without being secured by any Magistrate."
He also recommended to the assembly that "since it is become more
dangerous to settle our Western Frontier," those who braved the dangers
there should be allowed "not to pay Publick Taxes for some years after
their first settlement."[69]

By early January 1756, work on Fort Johnston and the new frontier post
of Fort Dobbs was proceeding, although the colony still lacked proper
artillery. The province's backcountry had seen few Indian attacks, which
Dobbs attributed to the efficacy of Waddell's company at Fort Dobbs and
friendly Catawba Indians nearby.[70] At the same time, some North Carolina
troops remained at Fort Cumberland, although paying and providing
for them proved challenging.[71] Later that winter, Dobbs had to admit
the difficulty of getting men to serve in the militia, or even to muster on
occasion. To avoid being drafted by the colony, some men would "fly to
the swamps and are concealed by their friends and Neighbours," as were
deserters from the provincial companies. Most of the militiamen were not

Re-created soldiers' barracks at Fort Dobbs State Historic Site. Troops would have occupied huts like this prior to the completion of the fort in 1756. *Author photo.*

armed, and at Fort Johnston, "there is at present neither ammunition, arms nor cannon except a few ship guns unfit for service."[72]

Construction also progressed on the batteries at Topsail Inlet and at Core Banks, but still no cannon or military stores were in place. The governor was especially desirous of finishing the battery at Ocracoke, "by which all ships must pass who trade to Neuse, Pamplico & Roanoak rivers, upon which the Towns of Newbern, Bath and Edenton are situated." The harbor at Portsmouth, a new town located opposite the Ocracoke Bar, was exposed to enemy privateers sailing along the coast, which "could from their mast head see every vessel in the Harbour, and go in and cut them out, or destroy them." Dobbs also continued to advocate for a fort at "Cape Look Out Harbour," which he called "the safest harbour from the Cape of Florida to Boston."[73]

North Carolina's provincial officers worked over the winter to enlist men in the three companies authorized by the last assembly session and for the diminished company under Captain Dobbs that remained at Fort Cumberland. The Carolina troops expected to serve out of the colony in 1756, but colonial officials were unsure how to supply or pay them once they left. The governor reported to London that "we have no Cash and our paper [money] is of no use" outside North Carolina. Only by selling commodities abroad could money be raised to provision the soldiers, but this was always a difficult arrangement.[74]

On a grander scale, at the end of 1755, colonial and British military leaders took stock of their defeats of the past year and began to plan for the next campaigns. While Braddock's troops had marched to the Forks of the Ohio and disaster, other British commanders in North America had achieved little success as well. Forces under Lieutenant Colonel Robert Monckton captured Fort Beausejour in Nova Scotia in June, but the campaign under Massachusetts governor William Shirley to capture Fort Niagara was unsuccessful. Moreover, Sir William Johnson did not capture Fort St. Frederic on Lake Champlain as planned, although his provincial troops thwarted a French thrust at the southern end of Lake George in September.

Upon Braddock's death three days after his column was ambushed on the Monongahela River, Governor Shirley temporarily assumed the role of commander in chief of British forces in the American colonies. For military operations in 1756, Shirley suggested defending the Virginia and Pennsylvania frontiers and conducting two offensives in New York. The first expedition would attack the French at Fort Frontenac on Lake Ontario in order to cut off enemy supplies and reinforcements to the Ohio Valley. This operation would be launched from Fort Oswego, on the southern shore of Lake Ontario, with two regiments raised in America. The second thrust would be an attack on Fort Carillon (later called Ticonderoga) and Crown Point, both on Lake Champlain, with a force of New England provincial regiments. Meanwhile, in London, British authorities tapped a military veteran, John Campbell, Fourth Earl of Loudoun, to replace Shirley in command in America. Major General James Abercromby was to be Loudoun's second in command. Both men arrived in America that summer, along with several regiments of redcoats from the British Isles.[75]

In response to Shirley's request for military support from all of the American colonies for the 1756 campaigns, Governor Dobbs sent the three newly raised North Carolina companies to serve in New York on Lake Ontario and against Fort St. Frederic at Crown Point, along with Major Dobbs's company of thirty men at Fort Cumberland, all to act under the command of the governor's son. "General Shirley...desired that I might appoint a Field Officer to command those 4 Companies, and as my son had a command in the Regulars, and was consequently the Senior Officer, I appointed him Major," Dobbs explained. The company

FRENCH AND INDIAN WAR

MAP OF THE SCENE OF OPERATIONS.

The northern theater of operations during the French and Indian War. Carolina troops served at several posts in New York in 1756. *Lossing*, Harper's Encyclopedia of United States History, *1905*.

in Maryland seems to have proceeded to Albany by transport ship, while the men recently raised in North Carolina also made the long journey to New York by water. These four companies had a combined strength of about two hundred men, and were led by captains McManus, Grainger and Arbuthnot, along with Major Dobbs. Governor Dobbs praised the abilities of Captain McManus, who later received an officer's commission in the British regulars, but he said Grainger was in "no way proper for an Officer" and found Arbuthnot wanting in integrity.[76]

The Carolina companies began to arrive in New York in May. A Pennsylvania newspaper reported that "Captain Gifford [possibly Grainger] arrived [in New York] with a Company of the North Carolina provincials; and we hear that the other three Companies are hourly expected." The other companies, however, appeared several weeks later. During the second week in June, "two Sloops from North-Carolina, having on board Governor Dobbs's Son, Major Edward Brice Dobbs, and his two hundred North Carolinians," sailed into the waters around the city of New York. They had been "sent hither to assist in the Reduction of the Fortress at Crown-point," according to reports. "A day or two after [arrival] they disembark'd and encamp'd on Kennedy's Island," one of several islands near the mouth of the Hudson River used that year as a quarantine station, "to refresh themselves."[77]

Considering the trying logistical difficulties North Carolina officials met when trying to pay and supply their troops during the 1754 and 1755 campaigns on the Ohio, it is surprising that Governor Dobbs ordered the companies to New York. Perhaps because the colony had not come under direct Indian attack on the frontier by that point, Dobbs was willing to ship the troops northward. His sense of imperial duty may also have influenced him as well. Still, he advised Lord Loudoun in July that he "shall find great difficulties in procuring Provisions to sell at New York to pay the 4. Companies I have sent there, as there are additional charges not provided for, such as tents, camps, furniture, Batteaus, Provisions and ammunition." He asked the general to pay the Carolinians "if we cant send over in time what is necessary to pay our Troops…until we can send returns to New York when you shall be repaid." The governor warned Loudoun that without help from the British commander, "we shall be obliged to disband our troops before the Assembly meets" in September, and if so, "must turn over the private men to other regiments, and bring back the Officers to raise men here, if more are wanted."[78]

The colony tried selling "Provisions & Commodities" at New York and in the West Indies, then using the hard money for supporting the troops, but this was a lengthy and complex process. Dobbs "wrote to Genl Shirley acquainting him with [the troops'] distressed situation on account of our irregular remittances and desired he would advance £500 sterling to pay them," which he did. Once Loudoun took over command in New York, Dobbs had to "apply in like manner to his Lordship, who advanced the like sum of £500." Dobbs and the colony's officers seem to count on being reimbursed by Crown officials for these loans.[79]

Lord Loudon made his headquarters at Albany when he arrived on the New York frontier in late summer. Assessing the situation there, he immediately cancelled Shirley's plan for an attack on the French forts on Lake Champlain as unworkable, given its reliance on inexperienced provincial troops. Instead, Loudoun worked to improve the organization and discipline of his colonial regiments and the logistical support for his army. He also turned his attention to the scene of action on Lake Ontario.[80]

The British regiments Loudoun had dispatched to America did not arrive in Albany in time to bolster the garrison at Oswego. This position—actually three forts on Lake Ontario at the mouth of the Oswego River—threatened Fort Frontenac and French control of the Great Lakes and Ohio River Valley. This weak British outpost became the object of a French military campaign in 1756, under the command of Major General Louis-Joseph de Montcalm-Gozon. With a force of four thousand French troops and Indian allies, Montcalm attacked Oswego and its two-thousand-man garrison on August 10 and compelled the British to surrender the post after a four-day siege. Following the surrender, Montcalm had his army destroy the British works there.[81]

Loudoun had ordered the Carolina companies to support British operations at Fort Oswego in June or July 1756, but they were not at the fort when it was attacked and given up. Rather, Major Dobbs's men were some distance away, at the settlement of German Flatts along the Mohawk River (in modern Herkimer County, New York), about eighty miles from Fort Oswego. They were involved in logistical operations supporting the campaign at this post west of Albany. A report in the July 12, 1756 edition of the New York *Mercury* noted that the "four Independent Companies of North-Carolina" and other troops "were posted at Oswego, and the several Forts and Carrying Places between that Place and Schenectady [New York]."[82] A 1756 letter to George Washington shows that the companies were under the command of Major Dobbs in late July at German Flatts, which included defensive works around several buildings on the south bank of the river in the 1740s and known as Fort Herkimer. The British supported Fort Oswego by shipping supplies on the Mohawk from Schenectady to Lake Oneida and then on to their outposts on Lake Ontario. The North Carolina troops stationed at German Flatts guarded part of this crucial link in the British logistics chain. After the fall of Oswego, the Carolinians relocated to the main British base at Albany.[83]

In late September, Governor Dobbs received a letter from Governor Dinwiddie in Virginia with news from the northern theater, including

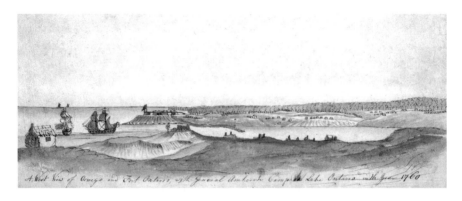

A view of the forts at Oswego on Lake Ontario, captured by French forces in 1756. Drawn by Thomas Davies in 1760. *Library of Congress.*

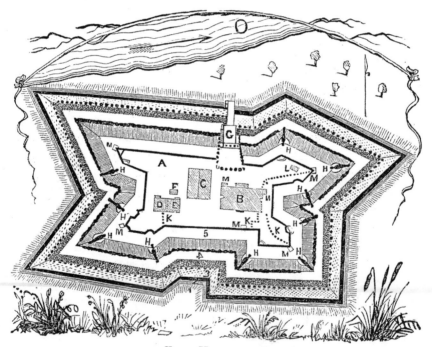

FORT HERKIMER.[1]

Fortified storehouses at German Flatts, New York, on the Mohawk River, called Fort Herkimer. North Carolina soldiers served here in 1756. *Lossing,* Field-Book of the Revolution, *1859.*

Oswego's capture. Dinwiddie had also heard that "your son was well, and believed his men were to be enlisted in the Royal Americans [as of 1756, the Sixtieth Regiment of Foot], and he to return for more Recruits" in North Carolina.[84] Major Dobbs's men were still at Albany in late October but could not be paid from North Carolina. Accordingly, Governor Dobbs ordered the company officers to try to get the men in the ranks to enlist in the Royal American Regiment or to have them enlist in the Forty-fourth Regiment of Foot, since there were no funds available to bring the men home. "The extraordinary expence in raising and transporting them to New York," Dobbs lamented, "has occasioned our contracting a considerable debt there, which we must repay."[85] Loudoun reported that he could not get the Carolinians to enlist in his regular battalions "without force," which he "thought better avoided." A number of them eventually did join the Sixtieth Regiment rather than return home.[86]

While Major Dobbs's blue-coated soldiers served with British forces far away to the north, military activities back in North Carolina continued in 1756. Efforts went on "briskly with our Fort at Cape Fear," although the heavy cannon for Fort Johnston still had not arrived from England. Dobbs hoped to have a fifty-man garrison for the fort, to be supported by local militiamen in case of an attack, as well as "a suitable number of men for the artillery." In July, the Privy Council of Great Britain directed that a "supply of Ordnance and Stores for the defence of Fort Johnson on Cape Fear river, and also the supply of ammunition for the defence of the Province of North Carolina" be sent immediately "for the better defence and security of the said Province." The council ordered desperately needed powder, ammunition and flints to be sent as well. "We are still here in peace with the Indians," Dobbs wrote to the Board of Trade in London. Still, settlers on the frontier were doubtlessly anxious, especially once Fort Oswego fell and allowed the French to supply the western Indians with arms and powder.[87]

Laborers continued to construct a two-sided battery at Portsmouth on Core Banks to protect the town's harbor and the Ocracoke Bar. This defensive work was built on piles five feet high to avoid spring tides, along with a wooden barracks. Dobbs hoped to get eight eighteen-pounder guns to cover the bar, and twelve twelve-pounders for the harbor's defense, along with "about 40 men to defend the House and Battery." A battery on Bogue Banks covering the town of Beaufort was also nearing completion, although a garrison and ordnance for it were still lacking. Dobbs thought these forts "may secure our four great rivers and chief Inlets." The governor again pressed London authorities to provide a permanent garrison—an independent company of regulars—for North Carolina's coastal defense, consisting of 120 men, but this suggestion was again ignored.[88]

Governor Dobbs remained convinced that "a large strong Fort [was] absolutely necessary" at Cape Lookout on the Outer Banks, to be built at British expense, "for the safety of the British Trade & Navigation to all these Northern Colonies, and also to the West Indies." Dobbs went so far as to draw up a plan for his proposed fort and sent it to Lord Loudoun. "I was obliged to act as Engineer myself & rub up my former knowledge in fortifications when I was in the Army," he wrote the general in New York, "and have accordingly drawn a plan for a square Fort to contain 2[00] or 300 men in time of Peace, and 500 in time of war...which will be sufficient to maintain it against any small squadron, or to be taken without a formal siege." He thought the location would be "a proper station for our Cruizers and stationed ships of war," which could easily patrol from the Capes of Virginia to Georgia. To "benefit...the whole Continent and British Trade," Dobbs concluded, the large fort "must be so strong and well garrisoned as to stand a small siege, for if the French should surprise or take it they would soon make it another Louisburg, or a Gibraltar, to disturb the whole Colony Trade even from Jamaica & the Leeward Islands." He urged Loudoun to refer the idea to British officials and requested a London engineer to begin the work. In the end, however, no fortress was built at Cape Lookout.[89]

In addition to constructing defenses, North Carolina military officers recruited for their provincial companies, as well as for Loudoun's regulars. Governor Dobbs suggested that his province might become "a recruiting Colony." North Carolina would raise, pay, "give cloathes, and Provisions, to the Officers & soldiers as long as they remain in the Province," and then they could be transported to wherever British commanders needed them. Once the men reached their new commands, they would be "taken off the Colony pay, and be paid by Britain during the Campaign," after which the private soldiers would be transferred to British regiments, while the officers returned to North Carolina to "recruit or new raise their Companies for next Campaign." Dobbs does not seem to have taken into consideration how the colony's poor financial state would allow them to entice recruits into service and uniform them, unless money was advanced by British authorities. In the end, this proved to be one of Dobbs's several impractical suggestions presented to his superiors for their consideration and quietly ignored.[90]

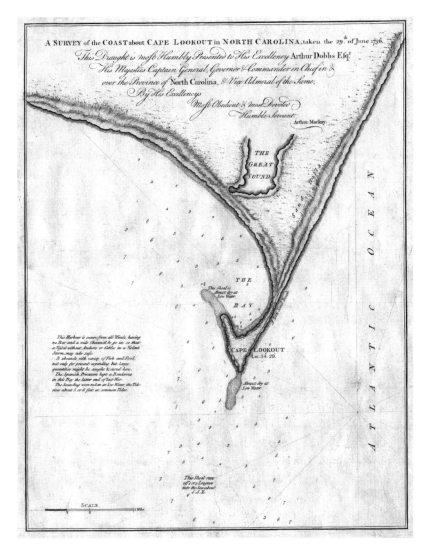

Cape Lookout on the North Carolina Outer Banks, from a 1756 survey. Governor Arthur Dobbs suggested fortifying this location to British officials. *North Carolina Collection, Wilson Library, UNC–Chapel Hill.*

That summer news of Indian troubles on the frontier began to reach Carolina leaders in the east. Along the Broad River and Catawba River there had been "several abuses and robberies committed by Strolling Parties of Indians," who were believed to be Cherokees "headed by some Fr. Indians and Perhaps two or three Northern Indians the French have Brought with

Tuckaseegee Ford on the Catawba River in western North Carolina. Cherokees made numerous attacks on settlers along this river during the war. *Lossing,* Field-Book of the Revolution, *1859.*

them." Dobbs thought that these intruders were trying to provoke settlers into attacking them, and thus instigate "a national war." He urged the settlers not to retaliate in order "to keep the peace."

To "put an end to the fears of the Inhabitants," Dobbs ordered two militia companies to patrol the region and to act under the command of Captain Waddell at Fort Dobbs. This officer was "in his person and character every way qualified for such a Command, as he was young, active and resolute," in Dobbs's estimation. The governor advised Waddell that the French were urging the Cherokees to "make war against us and Push them on to make these depredations." He also sent orders "to Cape Fear to send up One Hundred weight of Gun powder and four Hundred weight of Lead" for use by the friendly Catawba tribe, to help defend the backcountry.[91]

In response to fears of Indian raids on the frontier, the German-speaking Moravian settlers at the recently founded town of Bethabara (in modern Winston-Salem) worried about their exposed position in the western backcountry. Two groups of Cherokee Indians "behaved very badly" toward settlers around the town in May, "robbing and stealing from them." The Moravians noted that "many people are again leaving their farms for fear of the Indians."[92] In July 1756, the inhabitants there began more strenuous efforts to complete the stockade at the town for their defense. "It was decided to protect our houses with palisades," wrote one Moravian, "for if the settlers were all going to retreat, we would be the last left on the frontier and the first to be attacked." This renewed effort was begun after an increasing presence of Cherokees in the Carolina Piedmont earlier that year. "All work except the harvesting should be dropped until a palisade has been built around the houses," the Bethabara inhabitants decided.[93]

These roving Indian parties caused quite a few alarms in 1756. Moravians noted that summer that "families were leaving their farms and retreating" to the east, "leaving us on the frontier" vulnerable to attack. No known attacks were made by the Cherokee against the Moravians that year, despite their fears.[94]

By the fall of 1756, the assembly was in a state of apprehension for the safety of the frontier, particularly after hearing of the French capture of Fort Oswego. At the autumn legislative session, the lawmakers voted "£4000 to erect a fort to protect and secure the Catawbas, and to maintain

Map detail of the western backcountry, including the Moravian settlements and Fort Dobbs. Note Hughes Creek west of Bethania, where the Rowan County sheriff and family were attacked. *North Carolina Collection, Wilson Library, UNC–Chapel Hill.*

"A View of Bethabara," a contemporary depiction of the Moravian village surrounded by a stockade erected in 1756. *Moravian Archives Herrnhut, TS Bd.2.44.a.*

two companies to garrison that and another fort built last summer upon the frontier [Fort Dobbs]."[95] However, the assembly did not allow any funds or troops for service in the northern colonies, even after reading Lord Loudoun's circular letters to the several southern governors to prepare for the defense of "our Frontiers since the French have now free access by the Lakes to send troops to the Ohio, to attack us by their Indian Allies." The assemblymen also declined to send men out of the colony for military service "when our sea coast is quite exposed for want of a Company to garrison our Forts and Batteries which are now in a state of defense," the governor reported.[96]

The colony's agent in London, James Abercromby, explained to the Board of Trade two months after the assembly adjourned that North Carolina's previous efforts to grant men and money for the Crown's American campaigns "were all for extra provincial Services, and Operations without any Stipulation when and where to act." He also reminded the board "that poor as the Inhabitants of North Carolina are, their public Credit is greatly depreciated, by Taxations, beyond their ability for military service...their Armaments now on Foot must drop, however near the danger seems to Approach our Southern Colonies." In other words, the colony could not and would not raise troops for the benefit of other provinces that year, particularly since they worried about the dangers to their own frontier.[97]

After almost three years of warfare in America, Britons and colonial Americans had seen few successes by the end of 1756. In North Carolina, the assembly became reluctant to raise money and troops as it had earlier done, and concerns for the safety of the frontier became greater. To date, the conflict had been fought far to the north, on the Ohio River and the Great Lakes, but there were increasing signs that soon the war might come closer to home.

TURNING POINT: 1757

At the beginning of 1757, new plans and new leadership gave hope of success for British arms in the coming year. William Pitt had become the leader of the House of Commons, as well as secretary of state for the Southern Department, in December 1756. Except for a brief period in the spring of 1757, Pitt retained power and the direction of Britain's war efforts until October 1761. Upon his initial assumption of leadership in London, he lost little time before focusing on military preparations against France in both Europe and America.

Pitt sent a letter in February 1757 to the governors of the southern colonies, in which he urged them to "call together Your Council & Assembly & press them in the strongest Manner to raise with the utmost Expedition as large a Number of Provincial Forces as may be for the Service of the ensuing Campaign." These new levies were to be "over and above what they shall judge necessary for the immediate Defence of their own Province" and were to serve under Lord Loudoun's orders. No doubt much to the relief of Dobbs and the assembly, Pitt informed him that "the raising of the Men, their Pay, Arms, & cloathing will be all that will be required for this Campaign on the Part of the several Provinces[,] Measures having been already taken for laying up Magazines of Stores; and Provisions of all kinds at the Expence of the Crown."[98]

At the same time, British and colonial leaders in the South began to fear that the enemy would begin to exert more force against them in the near future. Lord Loudoun gathered Governors Dobbs, Dinwiddie, Sharpe and

William Denny of Pennsylvania for a meeting at Philadelphia on March 15, 1757, "in order to concert in Conjunction with them a Plan for the Defense of the Southern Provinces whilst the other Operations were carrying on." Loudoun informed the governors that he would provide one British regiment for southern service, along with the three independent companies of one hundred men each already in South Carolina.

William Pitt, secretary of state for the Southern Department from December 1756 to October 1761, urged the American colonies to support the British war efforts. *Library of Congress.*

Although the governors pledged to "use their best Endeavours with their several Provinces to raise and support" troops to act in conjunction with the regular forces, Dobbs could not have been overly optimistic about his own colony's willingness to cooperate. Nevertheless, he agreed to recommend to the assembly to raise two hundred additional troops as soon as possible, since the governors believed that South Carolina faced imminent attack from the French "either by Sea from St Domingo," or from their stronghold at Fort Toulouse, in modern-day Alabama. The North Carolina troops would march overland to Charles Town once raised and equipped and be supplied "with King's Provisions from the time they arrive in South Carolina," at the Crown's expense. Two hundred more North Carolina troops would be kept in service as well, at North Carolina's coastal defenses and at Fort Dobbs.[99]

Once Dobbs returned to North Carolina from the Philadelphia conference, he called the assembly to meet on May 13, to allow the four hundred troops to be raised. He advised Secretary Pitt that he would also call for "a Day of solemn Fasting & Humiliation" within the colony.[100] Once convened, the legislature agreed to raise two new companies of one hundred men each to serve outside the colony and £5,300 to maintain these men for six months or longer if necessary or at home in case they were unneeded in South Carolina. Dobbs, while no doubt pleased that the new companies were allowed, nevertheless reported to the Board of Trade a familiar lament: "We shall be under difficulties to pay them out of the Province."[101]

Soon after the assembly adjourned, Dobbs received a letter from Loudoun, with orders "to send the men as soon as they can be possibly ready to South Carolina and also to have the Militia along the Southern Frontier ready to go upon the first notice." Trouble with the French and southern Indians was clearly expected. All of these North Carolina forces were to serve under British lieutenant colonel Henry Bouquet, the commander of the First Battalion of the Sixtieth Regiment, the Royal Americans. This Swiss-born officer brought five hundred of his regulars and several hundred Virginia and Pennsylvania provincials to Charles Town by June. Dobbs ordered the colonial council members living in the Cape Fear region to "to send ⅔ of the Militia of the 4 Southern Counties to South Carolina upon the first notice" from either South Carolina's governor William Henry Lyttelton or Colonel Bouquet.[102] In late June, however, Lyttelton advised Dobbs not to send the North Carolina provincials to Charles Town, as there was no room to quarter them there once all of Bouquet's troops had arrived.[103]

Military preparations continued in the spring and summer of 1757. The colony's council suggested that the governor require militia officers to "Trayn and Exercise their several Ridgments and Companies" and to prepare their

Charles Town, South Carolina, in the late eighteenth century. *Lossing,* Field-Book of the Revolution, *1859.*

commands for active service. The militia organizations of New Hanover, Bladen, Duplin and Onslow Counties were specifically called on to have their men in immediate readiness for service in South Carolina. Powder and lead, always in short supply, were called for by the council as well.[104]

While striving to help defend South Carolina from an expected attack, North Carolinians also labored to secure their own province. In May, the council allowed the Moravians at Bethabara to establish "an Independant Company to consist of the Inhabitants…for their Defence from the French and their Indians" and commissioned Jacob Loesch as their captain. This maneuver allowed these German pietists to comply with the colony's militia laws, but only for defensive action. At the outbreak of the French and Indian War, the British Parliament had granted Moravians an exemption from military service.[105] Despite their aversion to war, the Moravians prudently continued to see to their own defense. They built a stockade on Manakes Hill, within musket range of and overlooking Bethabara, in October 1757, "for the sake of safety in case of attack by Indians." The German settlers observed that "many of our neighbors, driven hither and yon like deer before wild beasts, come to us for shelter."[106]

Governor Dobbs also tried to get recruits within the colony for British regular regiments but met with little success. Some recruiting parties from the Sixtieth Regiment attempted to enlist men in New Bern and Rowan County during 1757, but few men joined the ranks. Those who did often deserted immediately upon receiving their uniforms and bounties, and most of the inhabitants "despise our pay," according to one recruiter. With the war's active theaters so far away from North Carolina, it was perhaps no wonder that few men joined British regiments. Others may have been leery of joining given the lack of success British generals had experienced on campaigns up to that point or because of the long enlistment periods.[107]

In the west, Hugh Waddell and his company of provincials remained at Fort Dobbs. The previous year, the assembly commissioned Richard Caswell and Francis Brown to inspect the preparedness of the western counties for expected Indian attacks. They reported in May 1757 that Fort Dobbs was "a good and Substantial Building" and was an "Oblong Square" fifty-three feet by forty feet, "the opposite Angles Twenty four feet and Twenty-Two In height Twenty four and a half feet." The fort's blockhouse was made of horizontally laid oak logs and contained "three floors and there may be discharged from each floor at one and the same time about one hundred Musketts."[108]

The re-created stockade at Bethabara Historic Site, in Winston-Salem, North Carolina, with Manakes Hill in the background. *Author photo.*

The plans used to construct the fort have not been found, and no contemporary depiction of it is known to exist. It is possible that Governor Dobbs may have designed the fort, based on his military and engineering experience in Ireland and Scotland. Dobbs wanted a stockade fort to be built and defended with swivel guns—small muzzle-loading cannon typically mounted on blocks and aimed with a wooden bar by a gunner. Brown and Caswell found an imposing structure on the hill above Fourth Creek during their inspection. Outside the main log structure was a fosse, a defensive ditch less than two feet deep and about five feet wide, as well as an abatis, a barricade of felled trees or sharpened branches directed toward an enemy, which would keep attackers away from the blockhouse.[109] This stronghold was "beautifully scituated," and had a garrison of forty-six "effective men Officers and Soldiers," who were "appearing well and in good spirits." However, the two inspectors also noted that the western settlements "were in a Defenceless Condition except that part near Fort Dobbs" and recommended that additional forts be constructed including one near the Catawba Indians.[110] The fort for the Catawbas was started in 1757 with funds already allocated by the assembly but not finished.

In November 1757, the provincial assembly met again, in New Bern. The colony once more took up the issue of aid for the Crown's war efforts, especially for the next year. At this point, the assemblymen knew that the British Parliament had granted a sum of £50,000 to reimburse the military expenses of Virginia and the Carolinas, "upon account of the difficulties we lie under in supporting our forces when sent out of the Province," according to Governor Dobbs. He implored the representatives to "contribute with zeal our Contingent towards the support of the Colonies and our own security, as well upon account of the security of our western Frontier." He also desired to "secure the Forts upon the Sea coasts, which may enable us, to have Forces in readiness, and to spare when demanded for the security of South Carolina."[111]

William Pitt also encouraged the southern colonies to do their utmost in the fight against France and its Indian allies in 1758. He expected Pennsylvania, Maryland, Virginia, North Carolina and South Carolina to furnish "a body of several Thousand Men, to join the King's Forces in those parts, for some offensive Operations against the Enemy." Pitt asked the colonies to put "as large a Body of Men…as the Number of…Inhabitants may allow" into disciplined regiments, to be ready to participate in the campaign of 1758 no later than May 1. Aware of the previous difficulties that faced imperial authorities in getting the southern provinces to assist the Crown's war effort, the British sweetened the deal to encourage the various assemblies to vote more soldiers and supplies. Pitt advised the colonial governors that the king would furnish all troops raised for the war "with Arms, Ammunition, & Tents, as well as to order Provisions to be issued to the same, by His Majesty's Commissaries, in the same Proportion & Manner, as is done to the Rest of the King's Forces." Artillery would be provided for the southern operations as well. What the king expected, Pitt wrote, was for each province to raise troops, put them in uniforms and pay them.[112]

Despite these inducements, North Carolina's Assembly provided little to help the British Crown defeat its long time rival in North America. Representatives voted to keep active only three companies of fifty men each, fewer soldiers than the previous year. Dobbs surmised that the assembly refused to pay for more troops because the two hundred men it had agreed to send to South Carolina in 1757 were not needed. The frontier was still quiet that year as well, in part due to the two companies the colony maintained in the western counties. Owing to the assembly's parsimony, one of these companies would have to be transferred to "secure our Forts and Batteries on the Sea Coast."[113]

Lord Loudoun's reaction to what he perceived as North Carolina's dereliction of duty was severe. "I am sorry," he wrote to Dobbs, "to find your Assembly have now in the middle of the War reduced their forces without waiting to see what occasion there would be for them the ensuing Campaign." Loudoun thought it "impolitick" on the assembly's part, since the distribution of the £50,000 to be granted by Parliament to the Carolinas and Virginia "is to be given according to the Services that have or shall be done by each respective Province."[114]

As Loudoun no doubt came to learn from a frustrated Dobbs, the assembly's recalcitrance stemmed from a number of political issues within North Carolina that created tensions between the royal governor and the legislature. Relations between Dobbs and the lower house, which consisted of elected members from each of the colony's counties and several towns, had been marked by cordiality and cooperation for the first several years of the governor's administration. By the end of 1757, however, the assembly and the governor clashed at almost every session. Matters of the king's prerogative, paper currency, property titles, quitrents due to wealthy landowners, the colony's judicial system and land reform became stumbling blocks to effective government during the last few years of the French and Indian War. While these were not military matters (other than the issuance of paper money), the rancorous disputes they produced inhibited the cooperation needed to raise troops, money and supplies from 1757 until the end of the conflict.[115]

4

STRUGGLE IN THE WILDERNESS

Over the winter of 1757–58, Loudoun, Pitt and other British leaders could only look back at a string of defeats in the French and Indian War to that point. In addition to Braddock's disaster, the fall of Fort Oswego and the abandoned expedition against Crown Point, another stunning reverse for British arms occurred in August 1757 in New York. At Fort William Henry on the south end of Lake George, Lieutenant Colonel George Monro was forced to surrender the fort to besieging French forces under General Montcalm, the victor at Oswego the previous year. In an incident made famous by James Fenimore Cooper in *The Last of the Mohicans*, Montcalm's Indian auxiliaries massacred the wounded British and colonial soldiers left inside the fort as the garrison marched out toward nearby Fort Edward and then attacked the column outside the fort. The victorious French army burned Fort William Henry and then retired north to Fort Carillon (Ticonderoga), where it remained firmly positioned.[116]

Despite the lack of success to date, the British remained committed to prosecuting the war in America. Part of their plan for military operations during 1758 was another attempt to capture Fort Duquesne. Colonial officials and British military planners hoped that a successful attack on this French stronghold would deal a fatal blow to enemy Indian attacks on the Appalachian frontier by cutting off the supply of munitions that Indians received from the French. Pitt described the campaign as the "most expedient for annoying the Enemy, & most efficacious towards removing & repelling the Dangers, that threaten the Frontiers of any of the Southern Colonies on the Continent of America."[117]

In addition to this thrust into the wilderness where Braddock's 1755 campaign had met defeat, the British also planned operations to capture three key French positions: Fort Carillon on Lake Champlain, Fortress Louisbourg in Nova Scotia and Fort Frontenac on the eastern side of Lake Ontario. To coordinate these various military endeavors in America, the Crown replaced Lord Loudoun as commander in chief with Major General James Abercromby, a wealthy Scot who had entered the army in 1742.

To lead a mixed force of British regulars and provincial troops against Fort Duquesne in 1758, Pitt assigned fifty-year-old Colonel John Forbes, who would act as a brigadier general for the campaign. The Scottish-born Forbes, a veteran of the War of Austrian Succession (1740–48) and colonel of the Seventeenth Regiment of Foot, had been Loudoun's adjutant general in New York until March 1758, at which time he began preparations for his new assignment. From New York, Forbes wrote to Arthur Dobbs in North Carolina, requesting the colony's support for "operations to be carried on this ensuing Campaign to the southward of Pennsylvania." The new general declared that "from their known Zeal for the publick service," the southern provinces "will most chearfully and unanimously join in raising with the greatest Dispatch the Body of Men expected from them for the Defence of their own Confines and the Honour and support of his Majesty's Dominions in No. America." Given the history of limited support for military operations from all the southern colonies to date, Forbes's words were certainly overstated.

Nevertheless, Forbes asked that troops mobilized for service with his army "be able bodied good men, capable of enduring fatigue, and that their arms be the best that can be found in the Province." The general hoped that "none but those men who are good and that can be depended upon may be sent, as people either inclined to mutiny or desert would prove an immense Detriment to the service at so intricate a Time." He announced that soldiers raised in North Carolina would be paid four pence sterling while on the way to his army in lieu of provisions, "as Provisions cannot possibly be delivered to them upon their march." He also asked Dobbs to have the troops sent to Fort Cumberland by May 1, although he admitted that he was "a Stranger to the Southern Provinces, and therefore can make no guess of the Distance that the No Carolina troops will have to march in order to join the Army" by that date. In mid-April, Forbes moved to Philadelphia to better prepare for the coming march to the Ohio Country.[118]

Although Dobbs—ever the imperialist—wanted to support Forbes's upcoming operations, he was unable to do so and soon disabused Forbes of the notion that North Carolina would provide substantial assistance. With all of the financial and logistical difficulties North Carolina faced in raising, clothing and supplying military forces, the May 1 deadline was unrealistic. Dobbs hoped to increase the strength of the three companies the colony had on foot from fifty to one hundred men each but conceded that "it is impossible to raise more men in time and even these we have no credit to pay out of the Province." Still, Dobbs planned to use his "utmost Endeavours in promoting the Glorious Cause we are embarked in of securing the Religious and Civil Liberties of Britain and these Colonies, and to get rid at once of our inveterate insatiable Enemies."[119]

The governor called the legislature to meet in New Bern, and its session began on April 28, 1758. The assembly did increase the size of the colony's three companies to one hundred men each to serve with Forbes, "and gave £10 Bounty to each able Volunteer to send them with Dispatch." Two of these companies sailed to Alexandria immediately with all soldiers then in the ranks, while three officers remained in North Carolina to enlist more recruits and follow on later. The third company intended for Forbes's campaign was in the area around Fort Dobbs, and traveled by land to Winchester, presumably on the Great Wagon Road and through the Shenandoah Valley. While these men were on campaign, Jacob Franks and an assistant acted as caretakers of the fort from June to November.[120]

All three companies with Forbes were under the command of Hugh Waddell, recently commissioned a major, since Edward Brice Dobbs was unable to continue serving in America, "being seized with a confirmed Rheumatism." The assembly also authorized two additional companies of fifty soldiers each to garrison the seacoast forts. Singing a (by then) familiar refrain to William Pitt, Dobbs complained that "the Misfortune of this Province is that we have no Cash, our paper Currency at great Discount, and though we can raise and pay Men in the Province, yet we have no Credit to pay them out of the Province even at 50 per cent loss." The governor had to write to General Forbes to advance the pay of the Carolina soldiers while they were on campaign.[121]

Although Dobbs got the number of men he requested from the assembly, it was not done without some grumbling among the representatives. They voiced their "inexpressible Concern" at being called on once again for military assistance to the Crown, when "the Inhabitants of this Government are so impoverished." There may also have been some resentment at having

While marching through the Shenandoah Valley of Virginia in 1758 to serve in Forbes's campaign, Carolina troops passed many fortified structures, such as the Timber Ridge Presbyterian Church in Rockbridge County. *Todd Hostetter photo.*

to incur expenses to serve in other colonies. "It is impossible for us to give such demonstrative Proofs of our Zeal and Ardour as we could wish!" the delegates told Governor Dobbs. "However," they continued, "notwithstanding the Indigency of the Country, we shall with Dispatch and Alacrity, prepare a Bill for augmenting the number of Forces now in the Pay of this Province, and transporting and paying them when joined to his Majesty's other Forces." The assembly also granted notes of credit in the value of £7,000 to support these troops and the garrisons of the coastal forts. After adjourning, the next meeting of the assembly was scheduled for November 1758 at Edenton, the colony's former capital on Albemarle Sound.[122]

While Forbes gathered his forces and supplies for his expedition to capture Fort Duquesne, British arms met with a devastating defeat in the summer of 1758. After assembling a huge host of over seventeen thousand British redcoats and provincials from New York and Massachusetts on the south shore of Lake George, General Abercromby moved his men north by land and water to attack the French at Fort Carillon. On July 8, the general ordered several costly frontal assaults on the strong French entrenchments outside the stone fort, which resulted in a bloody defeat for his troops, who suffered almost two thousand men killed and wounded. Although the British army still significantly outnumbered the enemy, Abercromby withdrew his

Sir Jeffrey Amherst, commander in chief of British forces in America beginning in 1758. *Library of Congress.*

troops to their former camps on Lake George. The defeated general was replaced as commander in chief by Lieutenant General Jeffrey Amherst later that year.

In August, fortune finally smiled on British arms in America. Lieutenant Colonel John Bradstreet led his army of 150 British regulars and almost 3,000 provincials from the site of Fort Oswego in a campaign on Lake Ontario against the French position at Fort Frontenac. After a two-day siege, the small French garrison surrendered, which allowed British forces to block much of the logistical support the French had previously been sending from Montreal to its troops and allied Indians in the Ohio River Valley.

Meanwhile, General Forbes moved his headquarters to Carlisle, Pennsylvania, in preparation for his army's westward advance against Fort Duquesne. The core of his command consisted of 1,600 regulars—the Seventy-seventh (Highland) Regiment of Foot under Colonel Archibald Montgomery and four companies of Colonel Bouquet's battalion of the Royal Americans—supplemented by over 5,000 provincials, including those from North Carolina.

Although Forbes came under intense pressure from a number of Virginians—particularly George Washington—to use Braddock's Road for his movement to the Ohio River, he instead decided to march across Pennsylvania, blazing a new road through the dense wilderness as his army left the settled part of the province near Carlisle. His route went through Shippensburg and then on to Fort Loudoun, Pennsylvania. True to form, the Carolina troops were late for the beginning of the campaign. Forbes apparently did not expect them, having been initially unaware that they were en route from Governor Dobbs. The two companies that landed at Alexandria had not yet joined Forbes troops by mid-June, and the army's quartermaster—sent from Forbes's headquarters to locate them and speed their march—called them "an Army in the Clouds. I never expected them and if we had them they are good for nothing."[123]

Interior view of the re-created Fort Loudoun, Pennsylvania. North Carolina provincial soldiers encamped nearby while serving with General Forbes in 1758. *Doug Raines.*

Once the Carolinians eventually disembarked at Alexandria, they proceeded under their officers, Major Hugh Waddell and Captain John Paine, over the Blue Ridge Mountains to Winchester. From this valley town, the companies marched north to Fort Frederick, a stone fort with thick walls built by the colony of Maryland on the north bank of the Potomac River in 1756, about twenty miles west of Hagerstown. This post, unusually strong for a frontier fort during the French and Indian War, had four bastions, each of which probably mounted some artillery. Arriving there on July 11, 1758, the 110 Carolina troops were expected to assist in constructing a road from Fort Frederick to Fort Cumberland, around forty-five miles to the west.

Shortly after Waddell's troops reached Fort Frederick, nine North Carolinians deserted, evidently finding road work not to their liking. Major Waddell quickly sent out a detachment of his more reliable men to overtake and capture the fugitives. Coming upon them in the forest, the soldiers sent to capture their former comrades met with "the greatest Resistance" and had to fire a volley to subdue them. One of the runaways was killed and four

Major Hugh Waddell's North Carolina soldiers served briefly at Fort Frederick, Maryland, in 1758, along the Potomac River. *Doug Raines.*

captured during the brief mêlée, and the rest presumably escaped. Waddell's men did not stay long at Fort Frederick before marching north along the road east of Wills Creek to Fort Loudoun, Pennsylvania, where they were to be outfitted for the campaign. They left four ill soldiers behind in Maryland.[124]

On July 20, Waddell's ragged companies reached Fort Loudoun. This log fort had been built two years earlier on the west branch of Conococheague Creek, near Shippensburg, and most of the troops camped outside its walls. The fort was "a poor piece of work," according to a contemporary description, "irregularly built, and badly situated at the bottom of a hill subject to damps and noxious vapors."[125]

Ninety-six Carolinians, "including countless invalids," remained in the ranks by the time the companies arrived there. Indeed, North Carolina's troops sent to accompany Forbes were not an impressive command at this point. One observer said they were "in…absolute want of everything," particularly arms, tents and camp equipage. Maryland's governor Horatio Sharpe saw some of Major Waddell's men, probably at Fort Cumberland or Fort Loudoun, and wrote of the "beggary and desertion of the North Carolina Forces." Colonel Bouquet, who served as Forbes's second in command for the expedition, encountered some of Waddell's men in July and found them in "a pitiable condition," lacking "health, uniforms, and everything. I have never seen such misery. I believe they are good only for eating our provisions or guarding a fort." His conclusion that colonial officers "haven't an idea of service, and one cannot depend on them to carry out an order" may have been made with the North Carolina cadre in mind.[126]

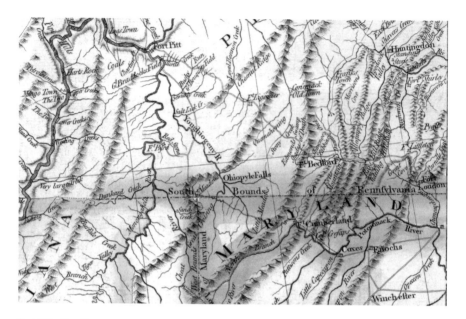

In 1758, Carolina troops served in Maryland and Pennsylvania, shown in this 1778 map detail. The soldiers marched from Winchester to Fort Loudoun and then on the Forbes Road to forts Lyttelton, Bedford and Ligonier, before helping to capture Fort Duquesne (shown here as Fort Pitt). *North Carolina Collection, Wilson Library, UNC–Chapel Hill.*

Similarly, Forbes had a dim view of provincial soldiers in general. These troops were "a gathering from the scum of the worst of people" and their officers typically "an extreme bad collection of broken innkeepers, horse jockeys, and Indian traders."[127]

The company from western North Carolina finally reached Winchester in September with forty-six men, having marched north from Fort Dobbs under Captain Bailie through the Shenandoah Valley. They proceeded into Pennsylvania and seem to have reached the main force by early October. Waddell's three united companies served in a brigade of provincial troops, including those of Maryland, Delaware, Pennsylvania and Virginia, all commanded by Colonel George Washington, who joined the army's march in late October.[128]

While the Carolinians trudged toward Fort Loudoun, which Forbes himself reached in early September, the general's campaign against the French was dealt an unexpected blow on the fourteenth of that month. An advance party of Forbes's army consisting of about 850 regulars and provincials under Major James Grant of the Highlanders made a reconnaissance march to the environs of Fort Duquesne. Grant also intended to attack enemy Indians camped outside the fort in retaliation for their raids against settlers and British detachments. Included in this excursion were thirteen men of the North Carolina troops.

Despite being undetected by enemy scouts as his soldiers approached Fort Duquesne, Grant foolishly surrendered the initiative and lost the element of surprise. After burning an outbuilding near the fort, the British force awaited an attack from the enemy Indians, which soon followed. Some French provincial troops from within the fort led by Captain Charles-Philippe Aubry quickly followed the warriors. Grant made the unusual decision to have the regulars play their fifes and drums, hoping to lure the garrison's troops to attack him on the wooded hills beyond the fort in a traditional battle. Grant put 250 Highlanders on his left and 200 Pennsylvanians on his right while the center was composed of men from the Sixtieth Regiment and the remaining provincials. The French and Indians struck the British position from the front and on both flanks, which were unsecured. A French witness to the battle wrote that "the shooting was very brisk during half an hour." The Carolinians and other provincials, all under the command of Major Andrew Lewis of Virginia, "concealing themselves behind trees and the brush, made a good defense; but were overpowered by numbers, and not being supported." Soon Grant's force was defeated with heavy casualties and thrown into great confusion, and both Grant and Lewis were captured. The British suffered 335 men killed, including 4 North Carolinians, and most of the dead were scalped. Pursued by hostile Indians for about three hours, the survivors fled to the new post at Loyalhanna, built fifty miles to the east.[129]

Although George Washington was not at this battle in front of Fort Duquesne, he wrote a lengthy (and critical) report of the fight from the British camp at Raystown, on September 25:

> *Major* [James] *Grant of the Highland-Battalion, with a chosen detachment of 800 men, marched from our advanced post, at Loyal Hannan, for Fort Duquesne, what to do there (unless to meet the fate he did) I can not certainly inform you: however to get intelligence and annoy the enemy, was the ostensible plan. On the 13th in the night, they arrived near that place, formed upon the hill in two columns, and sent a party to the fort to make discoveries, which they accomplished accordingly, and burned a log-house not far from the walls without interruption: stimulated by success the major kept his post and disposition until day, then detached Major* [Andrew] *Lewis, and part of his command 2 miles back to their baggage-guard, and sent an engineer with a covering*

party in full view of the fort, to take a plan of the works, at the same time causing the Revile to beat in several different places. The enemy [t]hereupon sallied out, and an obstinate engagement began.[130]

In a second letter three days later, he wrote that the raid was "either a very ill-concerted or very ill-executed plan: perhaps both."[131]

Despite this setback, Forbes's main force proceeded to cut a road through the mountains west of Fort Loudoun. Waddell's Carolinians marched north through Cowan's Gap and over Tuscarora Mountain to the provincial outpost called Fort Lyttelton, a group of several structures surrounded by a log stockade. This road was "perhaps worse than any other upon the entire continent," in Washington's opinion, and wore out "the greatest part of the horses that have been employed in transporting the provisions" from Carlisle.[132]

Next, the soldiers crossed Sideling Hill and Ray's Hill, both difficult ridges to traverse, until they reached the Juniata River. At this crossing, Forbes's engineers built extensive log stockades on each side of the ford. The Carolina provincials no doubt camped here for at least a short time before proceeding west to Raystown, a camp where the British had constructed defenses (later called Fort Bedford) one hundred miles from Fort Duquesne. This fort was built in the summer of 1758 by provincial troops and was a five-sided stockade with five bastions and an eight-foot-deep ditch surrounding it. Several other smaller defenses nearby, to house troops and artillery, were constructed of logs. Bouquet and Forbes made this post a major encampment during the campaign. Moreover, it was located at the junction of the newly built Forbes Road and an older pathway south to Fort Cumberland and Virginia. The North Carolinians came to this wilderness crossroads as well, although the duration of their stay is unknown.[133]

From Raystown in early October, Waddell's men headed west. The troops had to cross two significant ridges, the Allegheny and Laurel. The Carolinians marched through Rohr's Gap and then came to the fort (later named Fort Ligonier) at Loyalhanna, situated on a creek of the same name west of Laurel Ridge. This square fort had four bastions and other defenses outside its log walls. Three sides of the main fort were palisades, while the fourth was made of wooden baskets or cribs filled with earth. The fort had considerable artillery as well. Surrounding most of the fort was a "retrenchment," a low wall of logs positioned on top of each other horizontally. This gave some protection to the camps of the numerous troops assembled there in the fall of 1758.[134]

French and Indian forces attacked the strong British post at Loyalhanna (Fort Ligonier), in western Pennsylvania, where North Carolina troops were stationed in the fall of 1758. *Fort Ligonier photo.*

Major Grant's late September foray against Fort Duquesne had alerted the French garrison there of the looming British threat coming at them from across the rugged mountains to the east. In an effort to thwart Forbes's deliberate advance with a preemptive strike of their own, about six hundred French soldiers, Canadian militia and allied Indians—Delawares, Shawnees and Mingos—under Captain Aubrey set out from Fort Duquesne to attack the British position at Loyalhanna Creek, which was still incomplete. On October 12, a rainy and blustery day, the French and Indians suddenly attacked the British defenses, manned by 1,500 redcoats and provincials under Colonel James Burd of the Pennsylvania Regiment's Second Battalion. It was a powerful, unexpected assault that lasted three to four hours. The unanticipated attack began with the French overrunning the camps of the Maryland and North Carolina troops outside the fort. The Carolinians were startled by the French and were sent "fleeing for the main retrenchment, which they only reached just in time."

The French and Indian force remained near the fort overnight, and the garrison responded only by firing the fort's cannons at the enemy. "I played upon them with shells," Colonel Burd reported, but this officer made no other effort to attack the French. The fort's defenders suffered sixty casualties, including three North Carolinians listed as "missing" after the fighting, presumably killed or captured in the initial attack. The outnumbered French and Indians retreated, unmolested by the garrison, taking the camp's horses with them and hundreds of cattle as well. Forbes arrived soon thereafter, followed by Washington and some of his Virginia troops.[135]

The French at Fort Duquesne launched a second attack against the fort at Loyalhanna in early November, driving off much of the remaining cattle and hogs there in an attempt to cripple Forbes's supply situation. This foray was repulsed, but it highlighted the British army's precarious position—they were far from their logistical base and still fifty miles from their objective as winter approached. The British general—suffering from the illness that would eventually claim his life the following year—began to despair that the army would not take the fort that year. He described his force as one "composed of raw undisciplined troops, officer and soldier, newly raised and collected from all parts of the globe, from the Highlands of Scotland, Germany, etc., to…[North] Carolina."[136]

After some debate among his subordinates, Forbes decided to push most of his army across the high Chestnut Ridge and attack Fort Duquesne, leaving about six hundred men to guard Loyalhanna. It is unclear how many of Waddell's men were involved in this final operation against Fort Duquesne, although it is possible that part of them remained at Loyalhanna. Some North Carolina soldiers under Waddell did in fact serve in Colonel Washington's advance party, moving ahead of Forbes's main column to cut a path through the thick woods and acting as scouts. Waddell—along with his second in command, Captain John Paine—and his men were "employed in all reconnoitering parties" and "dressed and acted" as Indians. As the British worked their way through the wilderness, the weakened French force at the Forks of the Ohio—only three hundred men were present—decided to abandon Fort Duquesne, which they burned on November 23. The following day, the lead elements of Forbes's command entered the charred ruins, which Forbes renamed Fort Pitt. After two previous campaigns to drive the French from the Forks, the British and Americans had finally succeeded. The service of Waddell's troops with Forbes in 1758 was also the last time North Carolina soldiers served in a northern campaign.[137]

A fascinating incident occurred as General Forbes's column approached Fort Duquesne that affords a rare look at an individual North Carolina soldier during the French and Indian War. Forbes offered a "reward of Fifty Guineas and another Officer [offer] of Four Hundred Guineas" to any soldier who captured "an Indian Prisoner," who could be interrogated back at the British camp. Soon thereafter, while serving in the advance party with Colonel Washington, Sergeant John Rogers of the North Carolina forces "did take an Indian Prisoner in Novr 1758 who gave satisfactory Intelligence." Rogers later stated that he had acted "to distinguish his Zeal for the Public Service at the Hazard of his life." Dobbs later wrote proudly that "General Forbes' whole dependence for intelligence was upon the Carolina & Maryland Provincials, all others having failed in taking a Prisoner." Apparently only three Indian prisoners were captured around Loyalhanna, and their information about the weakness of the garrison at Fort Duquesne persuaded Forbes to press on and capture it before winter set in.[138]

Unfortunately, Forbes died in March 1759—before Sergeant Rogers received his prize. After petitioning the North Carolina General Assembly in the spring of 1760 for the money he never received, the legislature "resolved that the [petitioner] be allowed for his said Service twenty pounds Proclamation Money and that the same be paid out of Tax for Contingencys." This amount, however, was far below the value of the reward Forbes had announced during the campaign's last few weeks.[139]

To follow up on the success of 1758—the fall of the French fortresses at Louisbourg, Duquesne and Frontenac—Secretary Pitt in London urged all of the American colonies to aid the British war efforts in the following year, imploring them "to exert their whole Force upon this critical Emergency." The Crown once again expected the southern colonies to raise troops "for some offensive operations there," in cooperation with the king's forces. The British army would supply North Carolina's men with arms, ammunition, tents and provisions.[140] Although Pitt had written to Arthur Dobbs with these instructions on December 9, 1758, the governor did not receive the secretary's letter until early April 1759. Scrambling to make up for lost time, Dobbs and the council met at Wilmington on April 13 to convene the colony's assembly, but he worried that the long delay in receiving Pitt's letter would make it difficult for the colony to enact the appropriate legislation. "It will take time to raise and compleat any additional Troops which can be of no service Northward where the Campaign must be early," Dobbs informed Pitt. The governor did believe, however, that North Carolina could provide troops for a southern campaign later in the year.[141]

The assembly met "upon the shortest notice" on May 8 at New Bern, "in order to raise Men for his Majesty's Service pursuant to his Orders." To Dobbs's chagrin, the representatives did not pass a bill for assisting the

Crown's military efforts after fighting with the governor over issues regarding the royal prerogative and the rights of the Colonial Council. Dobbs dissolved the assembly in frustration. "I hope by the blessing of God we shall soon after this campaign have a glorious peace, and then His Majesty will have no great Demands upon this Province," he wrote the Board of Trade. The "Aid Bill" Dobbs rejected would have lowered the bounty for new recruits from ten to five pounds, which would have made recruiting difficult. "Had the Bill passed as proposed," the governor surmised, "it would have been of no Service to his Majesty." The colony still had two companies of fifty men each on foot, which Dobbs generously offered to send to the North, "but then we shall have none left to defend our Forts." He wrote Pitt that he was "extremely sorry I have not been able to cooperate farther in the glorious Plan of securing the British Empire in America," but the lower house of the contentious assembly would not budge.[142]

The service of Waddell's soldiers on Forbes's 1758 campaign to capture Fort Duquesne was perhaps North Carolina's most successful military effort during the entire French and Indian War. It also marked the last time the province sent men or money to assist British operations in the North, despite repeated requests from governors and generals to do so. Instead, the war had come to the North Carolina frontier, which led Carolinians to focus on their own safety and defenses.

5

THE CHEROKEE WAR

North Carolina's Assembly declined to send soldiers north in 1759 because it feared that the war was coming closer to its own province. Carolinians were particularly wary of the Indians across the western mountains, the Cherokees. One of the strongest Indian groups in the American Southeast, the Cherokee people lived in groups of towns and settlements in the western Carolinas, northwestern Georgia and what is now eastern Tennessee. In 1755, the Cherokee population was about 8,500, including 2,500 to 3,000 warriors—a formidable force. There were perhaps three to four dozen of these independent towns in the 1750s. Anglo Americans delineated the Cherokee into several groups based on geography. The Lower Towns were primarily in the upper Keowee River watershed of South Carolina, while the Middle Towns were in the western mountains and valleys of North Carolina, mostly along the Little Tennessee River. Across and on the western face of the Smoky Mountains were the Overhill Towns, remote from white settlements and, at times, influenced by the French. Additionally, the Valley Towns were to the south, at the headwaters of the Hiwassee River.[143]

The various towns of the Cherokee were rarely united in the realm of diplomacy with European powers, American colonial officials and other Indian groups. For many years, they attempted to avoid constricting alliances with other peoples. Some favored the British and looked for help in the form of redcoats to defend against attacks by hostile Indians (often prompted by the French in Louisiana). Others, particularly those of the

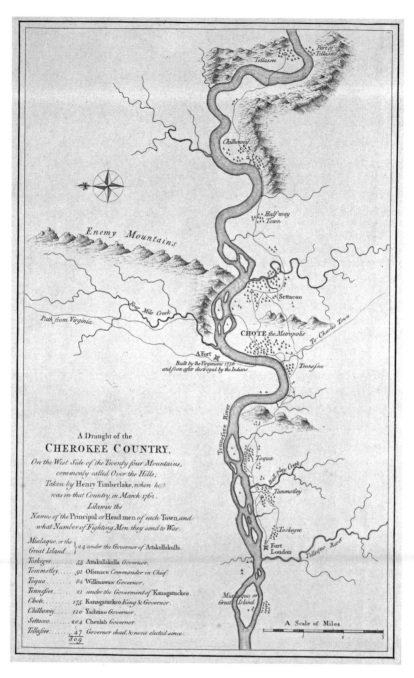

"A Draught of the Cherokee Country…" from 1765. *Colonial Williamsburg Foundation, Museum Purchase.*

Overhill Towns, were more apt to favor French advances, particularly by 1758, when South Carolina halted shipments of gunpowder to Cherokee towns. Other Cherokees traded with the Spanish on the Gulf Coast and at St. Augustine. For many years, the Cherokees were not required to choose among European powers (and their American colonies) for alliances, but by the 1750s, this tenuous position became difficult to maintain. Moreover, the area of Cherokee towns was in a state of transformation. Expanding Creek settlements to the south put pressure on the quantity of game and the expanse of hunting lands. To the north, Overhill Cherokees began to move up the Holston and Clinch Rivers into southwestern Virginia, a strategic travel and trade junction that Virginians were just beginning to settle. Trails and rivers leading south from Virginia into this region increased its potential to become a place of conflict.[144]

Prior to the French and Indian War, both Virginia and South Carolina had been in commercial competition with each other among the Cherokee villages. These traders tried to cut others out of this lucrative business, and at times, the colonies entered into separate negotiations with the Cherokees for trade and land concessions in return for military assistance. In an effort to resist the power South Carolina traders had over them, Cherokees led by Attakullakulla (called "the Little Carpenter" by the colonists) attempted to develop closer ties to Virginia for their trade goods and met in a conference with them at the Catawba town on the Broad River in North Carolina in February and March 1756. There, the Cherokees agreed to provide warriors to help Virginia defend its frontier in exchange for arms, gifts and a fort to be constructed for them in the Overhills region, at Chota on the Little Tennessee River.[145]

North Carolina had fewer commercial ties with the Cherokees, but its representatives attended the Broad River conference because the colony desired Indian lands across the Blue Ridge Mountains. As a way of securing the trade link with the Cherokees and "protecting" them from French influence, South Carolina constructed a small log bastion called Fort Prince George near Keowee and garrisoned it in 1753. Later, South Carolina constructed a second fort deep in Cherokee territory (in the Overhill Towns) on the Little Tennessee River and named it Fort Loudoun. A garrison of British regulars from the South Carolina Independent Company under Captain Raymond Demere occupied this remote palisade fort upon its completion in 1756.[146]

North Carolinians began to feel the sting of war on the frontier by the end of 1758. The Cherokees had often traveled through western North

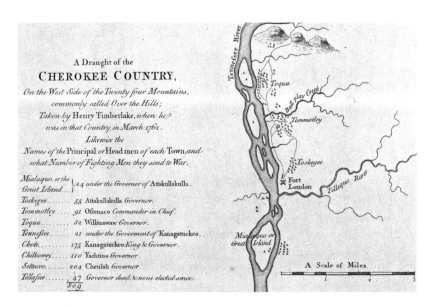

Detail of "A Draught of the Cherokee Country..." from 1765, showing the isolated Fort Loudoun in modern Tennessee. *Colonial Williamsburg Foundation, Museum Purchase.*

Carolina during their service with British forces in Pennsylvania and Virginia. In fact, George Washington provided a military escort for a party of Cherokees and "northern Indians" in October 1757 as they traveled south to Fort Dobbs. By the end of 1758, however, these Indians of the southern Appalachians had turned hostile toward the southern British colonies. The Cherokees had grown irritated and alarmed at the encroachment on their lands by American colonists who cleared the backcountry for their farms and intruded on Cherokee hunting grounds. Many Cherokee Indians complained to colonial officials about the fraudulent practices of white traders as well and grew frustrated at the delay of colonial officials implementing the terms of the Broad River treaty. In particular, Virginia failed to provide a garrison for the fort at Chota after construction. In addition, Shawnee and Creek Indians, along with French agents from Fort Toulouse in Alabama, traveled among the Cherokee towns in order to alienate the Indians from their eastern white neighbors.[147]

Despite attempts at continued trade and peace negotiations, tensions built up too high to avoid open conflict, even with the efforts of Attakullakulla and others to do so. As historian John Oliphant has observed, "The Cherokees wanted to safeguard their territory and autonomy," but South Carolina was "bent on subjugation and expropriation. The Cherokees saw themselves as equal allies whose sacrifices deserved presents and cheap trade goods." Whites more often than not regarded the Indians as "mercenaries: useful but contemptible auxiliaries, whose aid should be purchased as cheaply as possible, and if necessary by deceit."[148]

In this situation, British and colonial authorities worried that the strained relations between whites and Cherokees would ignite into open warfare. They urged backcountry inhabitants not to attack or threaten the allied Cherokees as they traveled to and from British forces in the north and their southern towns. In July 1758, for instance, Virginia's new executive, Lieutenant Governor Francis Fauquier, wrote to Forbes that "all possible care is taken that the Cherokee and all other Indians are civilly and kindly treated in their Passage thro' our back settlements." He also noted that the Indians themselves provoked some of the trouble. "Their behavior on some occasions," Fauquier reported, "has been so extremely provoking, viz by stealing horses, forcibly taking all provisions out of the poor inhabitants houses, even cutting their beds to pieces for the sake of carrying off the ticks, and supporting these outrages by arms." Angered, settlers fought back, "and some skirmishes ensued." Likewise, Washington concluded that Indian auxiliaries serving with Crown forces would "do mischief to the inhabitants in their return home (as some have done) if they leave…in an ill humor." Forbes called them "scoundrels," known for their "infamous behavior" and insolence if they did not receive suitable presents from colonial officials.[149]

The concerns of Fauquier, Washington and Forbes were not misplaced, particularly by the end of 1758. In the fall of that year, white settlers killed over thirty Cherokees near Winchester who had been serving with Forbes's British forces in the North. Similarly, backcountry militiamen attacked and killed a small party of Cherokees traveling through the Virginia frontier region in Bedford County in 1758 after the Indians had slaughtered stolen cattle. These and other similar incidents on the Anglo-Cherokee frontier enraged the Indians and ultimately led to retaliatory attacks in the western reaches of Virginia and the Carolinas.[150]

In April 1758, Indians, probably Shawnees, killed settlers in Halifax County, Virginia, near the border with North Carolina, along the Mayo and Irvine Rivers. The lower house of the assembly received a petition from Rowan County inhabitants in May 1758 "setting forth, That the Murthers lately committed on the Dann River hath occasioned the

The Dan River near Hanging Rock. Indians attacked settlements along this North Carolina river in 1758. *Jeffrey P. Oves photo.*

Inhabitants of the Forks of the Yadkin to leave their Settlements, &c., Praying the Continuance of Captain Bayley and his Company, or some other in his Room" at Fort Dobbs. Refugees continued to pour across the Yadkin River, heading east. Attacks like these led the backcountry Moravians to erect a stockade around their water mill and strengthen the palisade at Bethabara. "All the cabins in the fort have been filled with refugees," Moravians reported.[151]

Not all attacks on North Carolina's western settlers by hostile Indians were reported, but news of many incidents of frontier violence was heard across the colony. In April 1759, Cherokees from the town of Settico killed several settlers along the Yadkin and Catawba Rivers, and eight people were killed and scalped on Fourth Creek, a tributary of the former. On a fork of the Catawba, Indians murdered eight children of the William Morrison family that spring. The southern colonies were, in the words of British General Jeffrey Amherst, "exposed to the cruel and barbarous insults" of the Indians.[152] One North Carolinian reported in May 1759

Site of the 1755 Moravian water mill near Bethabara, North Carolina, fortified with a stockade during the war years. *Author photo*.

The Yadkin River at Shallow Ford, about ten miles west of Bethabara, where many refugees crossed the river fleeing Indian raids. *Author photo*.

that "there is many of the Inhabitants have already moved away and many more will go except some Means will be made Use of in order to secure them for they expect more of the same Nature daily."[153]

In May, Cherokees surrounded the house of the Rowan County sheriff near Bethabara, where he and his family were defending themselves. Somehow, Sheriff Hughes got word to the Moravians pleading for help, which prompted a party to ride to his house. Seeing the Moravians approach, the Indians fled into the forest, and Hughes's family was rescued. Not all were so fortunate. Later that month, Cherokees killed a hunter on the Tarrarat (Ararat) River, in the area of modern Mount Airy.[154]

In June 1759, the *Pennsylvania Gazette* reported:

> *According to Letters received yesterday from Gentlemen of Repute in Rowan County, in North Carolina...many horrid Murders have lately been committed by Indians, on the Yadkin and Catawba Rivers. The Number of People killed, in some Letters, are said to be 13 or 14, in others 17 or 18; and the Murderers are supposed to be Cherokees, tho' they may as well be Shawanese, or of those Indians who were prevailed on to quit the Ohio with the French Garrison of Fort Duquesne. Among the Killed are named John Snap, Thomas Ellis, Thomas, Adams, Daniel Holsey, and Joseph Rentford, in the upper Branch of the Yadkin; John Hannah, and his Family (supposed to be 7 in Number) near Fort Dobbs and Conrad Mull, on the Catawba River.*

Mull and his family had lived on the west side of the Catawba near Elk Creek since before 1750, north of today's Lenoir. Mull actually survived being scalped, but his wife and son did not. "Many of the inhabitants have already moved away and many more will go," wrote a correspondent of Governor Lyttelton in May.[155]

In response to the dangers on the frontier, many settlers fled their homes and traveled to Bethabara, as they had done the previous year. In the overcrowded Moravian town, typhus fever broke out among the refugees and inhabitants, and ten of the Moravians died of the disease, including the area's only physician. Armed sentinels kept a constant vigil for roving Indians outside the stockade. "Our hearts rest in childlike hope...our children are ignorant of the war and murder around them," one Moravian wrote at the time of the danger. The town of Bethania, founded about three miles away by Moravians in 1759, was settled in part due to the crowded conditions at Bethabara.[156]

Gravestone of Dr. Martin Kalberlan Bethabara, the Moravian physician who died during the 1759 typhus epidemic. *Author photo.*

The official colonial reaction to frontier Indian attacks was predictable: military operations in the backcountry and across the Appalachians to destroy the power and resources of the Cherokees. Three separate campaigns would be launched, primarily from South Carolina, in 1759, 1760 and 1761, the last two with the active support of British army regulars and other colonial forces—including North Carolina troops. "A peace with that misguided people," wrote General Jeffrey Amherst, "is only attainable by the sword."[157]

Outside the southern American colonies, 1759 was the "Annus Mirabillis" for Great Britain's military operations during the Seven Years' War. That year, British campaigns resulted in the capture of Fort Carillon in July by a force commanded by Amherst. General James Wolfe's army captured Quebec after a climactic battle outside the city's gates in September, in which Wolfe was mortally wounded during the fighting. In Prussia, a combined army of British and German forces defeated more numerous French and Saxon troops at the battle of Minden in August, while the British navy won a signal victory over a French fleet at Quiberon Bay off the coast of France in late November. With the loss of Quebec (compounded by the fall of Montreal the following year) the French lost control of much of their colonial possessions in North America and the ability to support their Indian allies with weapons, powder and trade goods. Nevertheless, British and colonial authorities in the South still found it difficult to defeat the Cherokees and only managed to do so at the end of 1761.

By the middle of October 1759, continuing reports of hostilities from the western borderlands alarmed Carolina leaders. South Carolina governor William Henry Lyttelton informed Arthur Dobbs that the "Cherokees were up in Arms" and had interrupted communications between Fort Prince George and Fort Loudoun. Lyttelton was preparing a military expedition into Cherokee country. He had written to Dobbs "to know what Assistance he could have from this Province" and asked the same of Virginia. Dobbs put several county militia organizations on notice for imminent duty and told them to ascertain "what Number each had who were ready and fit for service, and to have them ready in order to be draughted to send Detachments if necessary immediately to the Frontiers."[158]

Dobbs also commanded Hugh Waddell and his provincials at Fort Dobbs "to protect the Frontier Inhabitants" and mobilize the militia regiments of Anson, Rowan and Orange Counties if necessary. Dobbs sent Waddell a colonel's commission as well. All these forces, once assembled, were to cooperate either with South Carolina's expedition against the Cherokees or with Virginia troops. Dobbs ordered "a Supply of Barrils of Gunpowder and 4000 weight of Bullets, Swan Shot and Lead, & 1500 Flints" for the anticipated backcountry campaign. He could do no more until the assembly met at Wilmington in November, "which is the soonest they can attend," he informed Pitt in London. Warming as he wrote, Dobbs stated that "Virginia and the Carolinas should exert their whole force, enter into and destroy all the Towns of those at War with us." Additionally, he suggested that the colonial forces should make slaves out of all captured Cherokee women and children, transporting them to sugar plantations in the West Indies.[159]

Lyttelton planned to march an inexperienced force of militia, volunteers and provincials to the frontier via Fort Prince George and attack Cherokee villages in retaliation for the recent attacks. The governor demanded that the Cherokees hand over the "murderers" of the settlers and vowed to attack the Cherokee villages if denied. Some regulars of the British Independent Company stationed in South Carolina also joined Lyttelton's column, which included one thousand troops and artillery. In early December, his command reached Fort Prince George and encamped on the opposite bank of the Keowee River from the Indian village of the same name. The governor conducted tense negotiations with Cherokee leaders, while smallpox began to infect his soldiers as they waited in their wet camps. Lyttelton finally ended the anticlimactic campaign without fighting a battle or a destroying a native town. He and his weary soldiers began the long march back to Charles Town on December 28, after concluding a treaty with the Cherokees to bring to justice the warriors guilty of raiding the Carolina frontier. It was, in the words of Arthur Dobbs, a "peace without blood."[160]

In trying to assist Lyttelton's campaign, Dobbs was able to get the North Carolina Assembly to approve sending troops to South Carolina, but while they began to mobilize, Lyttelton concluded his treaty with the Cherokees. Waddell had raised some troops in the backcountry and tried to draft more men in Salisbury in the fall. Of the five hundred militiamen drafted to serve in this winter campaign, all but eighty of them deserted, and none reached Lyttelton's camp. "I Could not make a proper Number Turn out," Waddell complained to Governor Lyttelton on January 1, 1760, "but I shall Prosecute those Delinquents To the Rigor of the Law upon my Return. Nothing Could have Given me greater Pleasure Than Serving a Campaign under your Exc'y But as Matters have turn'd out I can't now Expect it."[161]

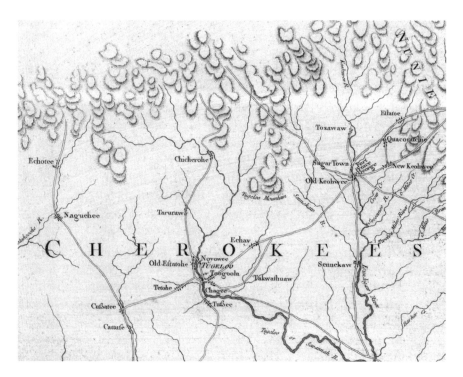

Map detail of Cherokee Lower Towns and Fort Prince George in western South Carolina. *North Carolina Collection, Wilson Library, UNC–Chapel Hill.*

Dobbs attributed this lack of zeal for the British cause to "their want of Education & Instruction, for want of schools and a pious Clergy to inspire them with Christian Principles." Calling Lyttelton's bloodless operation a success, he thought the Cherokees agreed to the treaty once they realized the Carolinas and Virginia were aligned to attack them. The Indians had been made "sensible that the 3 Provinces would join against them, which with the glorious Conquest of Quebec brought them to reason." In a final flourish of imperial enthusiasm, Dobbs told Pitt that after the many military successes in 1759, he hoped to see the "conquest of Mississippi and Mobile," the "opening [of] the Hudson Bay Trade" and the "conquest of the remaining [Caribbean] Sugar Islands in one Campaign." He also looked for "the Civilizing and converting [of] the Natives of this great Continent upon a confirmed Peace, and that His Majesty may die the greatest Prince in Europe." All of this would "secure the future peace of these Southern Provinces, which will prevent any future American Wars with the French."[162]

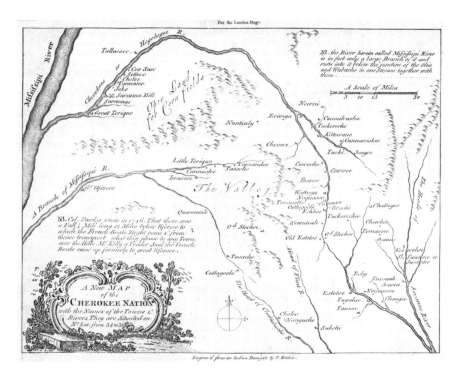

"New Map of the Cherokee Nation," produced around 1760. *North Carolina Collection, Wilson Library, UNC–Chapel Hill.*

Lyttelton's peace with the Cherokees did not last long. In February 1760, Indians attacked Fort Prince George, as well as the fort at Ninety-Six, South Carolina, that month and in March, in retaliation for the execution of Indian hostages by South Carolina authorities. They were goaded on by the French and Creek Indians to the southwest. Overhill Cherokees cut off supplies from reaching distant Fort Loudoun. By March 20, Indians began to fire on Fort Loudoun and those soldiers who dared to venture outside of it. Not all Cherokees sought a war with the colonies, but those who advocated violence carried out the raids. These attacks invited retribution on all Indians by whites, who rarely took the trouble to differentiate friendly Cherokees from those who were hostile. Hard hit by these attacks, Lyttelton called to Virginia and North Carolina for help and also to General Amherst in New York, to whom he requested that British regulars be sent to Charles Town without delay. Lyttelton left the colony a few months later to take up the governorship of Jamaica and was replaced with acting Governor William Bull II, who had opposed the recent foray into Cherokee country.[163]

Before attacking forts in South Carolina and Tennessee in 1760, a Cherokee party from Settico came to Fort Dobbs in February of that year—with the intent of destroying it and its thirty-man garrison. Colonel Waddell noticed a small party of Indian warriors moving in the woods around the fort, but scouting parties were unable to locate them when he sent them beyond the fort's defenses. On the night of February 27, Waddell heard "an uncommon Noise" coming from a nearby spring outside the fort. The colonel feared that it might be a ploy by the enemy "to draw out the Garrison" and ambush his soldiers, so he and Captain Bailie led eight men toward the disturbance to investigate.[164]

Waddell's small party "had not marched 300 yds from the fort when we were attacked by at least 60 or 70 Indians." He had ordered his men not to fire until he gave the command. Once the colonel concluded that all the Indians had discharged their muskets, he ordered his men to fire at close range "not further than 12 Steps" away from the Cherokee warriors, who "had nothing to cover them as they were advancing either to tomahawk or make us Prisoners." The Carolinians' muskets were "each loaded with a

Probable site of the 1760 skirmish at Fort Dobbs between Cherokee raiders and the garrison. The spring in the low area in front of the trees may be that mentioned in Waddell's report. *Author photo.*

Bullet and 7 Buck shot," which made their volley "very hot from so small a Number." The firing seemed to put the Indians into confusion. "I then ordered my party to retreat," Waddell reported, "as I found the Instant our skirmish began another party had attacked the fort." Once Waddell's detachment returned to the fort, "the Indians were soon repulsed with I am sure a considerable Loss." Waddell's own musket was shattered by an enemy bullet as he held it in his hands.

He estimated that the Cherokees suffered about a dozen killed and wounded, "and I believe they have taken 6 of my horses to carry off their wounded." The following day the soldiers "found a great deal of Blood and one dead, whom I suppose they could not find in the night." The garrison suffered two men wounded, "one of whom I am afraid will die as he is scalped, the other is in a way of Recovery." There was also "one boy killed near the Fort whom they durst not advance to scalp." There were no further attacks, as he expected the Indians "did not like their Reception." This skirmish was the only time Fort Dobbs was attacked during the French and Indian War.[165]

Indian violence continued against settlers on farms scattered across the backcountry. Reports circulated of an incident in which Indians cut the feet off a victim named William Shaw in late 1759, but he survived despite these grievous injuries. Frightened settlers again abandoned their farms and fled east of the Yadkin River.[166] Waddell sent powder from Fort Dobbs to Bethabara in February 1760, and Moravians reported that many local cabins were burned. In mid-March, "two men were killed at the bridge over the Wach [creek]" south of Bethabara, and two more were killed on Town Fork, in the northern part of the Moravian settlements. "Among our neighbors," recorded the Moravians' diary, "more than fifteen people were slain." Hostile Indian scouts roamed the woods around the towns, and their camps were close enough so that the watchmen could see the smoke from their fires.[167]

Along a tributary of Fourth Creek, near Fort Dobbs, Indians struck again in March 1760. A soldier named Robert Campbell and several others were involved in a skirmish with Cherokees at the house of Moses Potts in which Campbell received "Two Shot in [his] Back and the other Broke his Arm near his Shoulder and immediately [he] was tomahawked in Several Places & Scalp'd." Seven soldiers were reportedly killed and buried there.

In March, Indians were also seen in the new settlement of Bethania but were driven off by shots fired by the night watchman. In September 1760, warriors ranged the backcountry around Wachovia and later

Backcountry settlers fled east of the Yadkin River during times of Indian attacks. *Lossing,*
Field-Book of the Revolution, *1859.*

reported that they feared to attack Bethabara due to the ringing of the
town's bell and the sounding of the village horn at night.[168] A report of
an Indian attack reached Virginia's governor Francis Fauquier in late
March 1760, describing violence near the confluence of the Mayo and
Dan Rivers (at today's Madison, North Carolina), where "many Persons"
had been "taken and killed."[169]

The attack on Fort Dobbs and many other hostile incidents in the
western Carolinas were soon to be met by British and colonial forces.
In response to South Carolina's pleas for assistance in battling the
Cherokees on its frontier, General Amherst sent Colonel Archibald
Montgomery and most of his Seventy-seventh Foot to Charles Town.
Joining this regiment of red-coated Highlanders were four companies
of the First (Royal) Regiment of Foot. Major James Grant—who led the
disastrous reconnaissance against Fort Duquesne in 1758 during Forbes's
campaign—accompanied the troops as second in command of the
expedition, having been earlier liberated in a prisoner exchange. These

veteran soldiers began to arrive in South Carolina in early April 1760 and formed the nucleus of a renewed military effort to put an end to Cherokee depredations in the backcountry and to rescue Fort Loudoun, which was still under siege.[170]

Earlier in 1760, William Pitt had again written to the southern governors urging them to support Montgomery and South Carolina for the spring campaign. Governor Dobbs received the letter on March 27 and ordered the assembly to convene at New Bern on April 22, "it being impossible to meet them sooner." He promised Pitt to use his "most zealous endeavours to promote the raising of as many Men as We can in the short time we have to do it in upon this important Crisis." He also reminded Pitt that the colony would have to issue paper currency to "raise[,] cloath and pay" the North Carolina provincials and that "we can have no Credit to pay them when taken out of the Province…as we have no Specie here, nor Goods that will answer to remit it abroad."[171]

The April session of the assembly was a contentious one. The majority of assemblymen had grown tired of the repeated requests from Dobbs (and by extension, Pitt and the British government) for financial and military assistance for the war. Many of them tried to get the governor to agree to a quid pro quo: an exchange of military aid for their own political ends. Dobbs complained of "a tedious delay with many alterations, addresses and messages, for above thirty days without passing an Aid Bill." This led him to suspend the assembly for a day, in order to have the county representatives "reconsider" a bill on the colony's superior courts, which Dobbs disliked. "They endeavoured to force me to pass" their judicial bill "before they would grant an aid Bill," but this was "contrary to his Majesty's Instructions and a violent infringment of his Prerogative," a frustrated Dobbs complained to the Board of Trade.

By the end of May, the lower house tried to have the governor approve a measure—"crude and undigested," in Dobbs's opinion—to issue £12,000 in paper currency "without any Tax to sink the Notes" and to raise troops only "to defend the Province…against the Cherokees," not to support South Carolina or Colonel Montgomery's operations. "His Majesty was only to have an Aid of 320 [soldiers] added to 30 before in Pay," wrote Dobbs, and "Another Company of Fifty was to be Raised and these were Oblidged to Serve on the Frontier and not farther Act Against the Cherokees." Additionally, "three Companys more of one hundred Each were To be raised in Order to join and Assist the Virginians if any were sent against the Cherokees." A proposed enlistment bonus of only twenty shillings was far too little to attract enough recruits to participate in a campaign against the Cherokees that summer, in Dobbs's opinion. Furthermore, North Carolina had no arms available to issue to any new troops. The bill also provided money for an agent, Robert Jones, to act as the legislature's own representative in London, which the governor thought irregular and insulting to himself. Dobbs refused to sign the bill.[172]

Once Dobbs rejected "this Nugatory Aid," the legislators met as a "Committee of the Whole House," in which they "entered into Several Resolutions against [Dobbs] Equally False as Trifling," according to the governor. In an extraordinary scene, they locked the doors of their meeting room, "bound themselves To Secrecy" and refused to allow Dobbs to view the resolutions against him in the record. By the time that Dobbs rejected the bill and the assembly was dismissed without providing assistance for Montgomery's campaign, the British force had already reached Fort Ninety-Six.[173]

Montgomery's expedition had been directed by General Amherst to march into Cherokee territory beyond the post at Ninety-Six and "act against them offensively by destroying their towns, and cutting up their settlements." Amherst ordered this foray into the backcountry for the purpose of "punishing the Cherokee Indians for their perfidious breach of the Treaty of Peace which Governor Lyttelton lately concluded with them," although he failed to mention the murder of the Indian hostages by the South Carolinians. The British troops were to return to Charles Town after the operations on the frontier and were not to garrison forts or remain in South Carolina for purely defensive purposes.[174]

In March, 689 troops from the Royal Regiment and 684 men from Montgomery's Highlanders sailed for Charles Town from New York.[175] After landing near Charles Town, Montgomery and Grant marched their soldiers to Moncks Corner in "extremely hot" weather and reached Ninety-Six (which Montgomery called a "sort of fort") on May 24, 1760. About eighty South Carolina provincials and three hundred rangers accompanied the redcoats. On the way, wagons supplied by North Carolina joined the army at its camp at the Congarees, below the confluence of the Saluda and Broad Rivers. After being in South Carolina for less than two months, Montgomery reached a telling conclusion about the native enemy to the west—he saw that the Indians had been harshly dealt with by white settlers, traders and government officials, "and if they could tell their own story I doubt much if they are so much to blame [for the hostilities] as has been represented by the people of this province." Still, his orders were to attack the Cherokees, and he proceeded onward to the mountains.[176]

The British force experienced logistical problems in receiving provisions and supplies deep in the western wilderness as it marched toward the Cherokee Lower Towns. Even before he reached Fort Prince George in early June, Montgomery realized that the mountainous terrain and lack of troops from South Carolina added to the expedition's difficulties. South Carolina's governor Bull began to see that the rescue of Fort Loudoun might be better staged from southwestern Virginia, which was actually closer to the fort. Once the redcoats arrived at Fort Prince George on June 2, they attempted to surprise the important Cherokee town of Estatoe, in modern Oconee County, South Carolina. After a night march, the British attacked the town, from which most of the Indians had fled, and burned it. Montgomery's troops "then proceeded to their other towns which all shared the same fate." The British commander sent word to Cherokee leaders in the Overhill Towns that they should send representatives to treat for peace—or their towns would also be ravaged by the British force, which had returned to their camps near Fort Prince George.[177]

Fearful of a Cherokee attack in the mountains and low on supplies, Montgomery and Grant decided not to attempt the relief of Fort Loudoun. Both men thought the Cherokees were already defeated and would soon sue for peace anyway. However, when no enemy Indians appeared for negotiations at the army's camp, the British commanders began to prepare for renewed hostilities, although not a sustained operation. On June 24, most of the army marched northwest without its baggage or tents toward the town of Etchoe, located in the North Carolina mountains near modern Otto (nine miles south of Franklin, in Macon County). The terrain the army passed through was the most "difficult and strong" Montgomery had ever seen, with "innumerable" passes and gaps ideally suited for defense and ambush. A strong force of Cherokees had gathered nearby, as well as some Creeks and Choctaws from the far west and south. At a narrow pass in the mountains south of Etchoe, the Cherokees posted themselves "upon very advantageous ground," above the Little Tennessee River, which the troops had been following north.[178]

Colonel Montgomery advanced a ranger company of about fifty men ahead of his column to flush out any warriors in the thickets as his soldiers moved into the wooded defile. The Indians opened fire and drove

The rugged terrain near the site of the 1760 battle between Cherokee warriors and Montgomery's British army. *Christine I. Wilbanks.*

back the scouts, killing the rangers' commander as his men "infamously" fled. Next to go forward were the army's red-coated grenadiers and light infantry. While Indians took deliberate aim and individual shots at the British, these soldiers fired their muskets in platoon volleys at the concealed enemy, which was ineffective in forested terrain. British soldiers fell to the ground under the heavy Indian fire from the brush and thickets, and at times, the fighting was hand to hand. At least some warriors were armed with rifles rather than smooth bores, and their deadly accuracy dropped many of Montgomery's soldiers. "The savages indeed kept firing constantly upon us…[and] they did great execution," Montgomery wrote. The colonel brought up more men, deploying the Highlanders to the left and the First Regiment's soldiers to the right, as they tried to envelop the Indians' flanks with fixed bayonets. The Cherokees were hard pressed and fell back, some continuing to fire at the British and others running back to warn those in the town of Etchoe of the enemy's approach. Some Indians also attacked Montgomery's supply wagons in the pass and were driven off only after fierce fighting by a detachment of the Royal Regiment.[179]

One witness to the battle left a description of the fighting:

The Cherokees…shewed some judgement in taking possession of ground that was most advantageous to them…they had vastly their advantage of us with their rifle barreled guns, which did execution at a much greater distance than our musket; besides they fought in their usual way and we gave them our fire by platoons. Some of the Indians spoke English and gave us very insulting language.[180]

Although the British force suffered significant casualties in the engagement—seventeen dead, and sixty-six wounded—Montgomery's small army managed to enter and destroy Etchoe the day after the battle. "The Indians I fancy will not soon forget us," Montgomery bragged to Amherst in an "after-action" letter. He estimated Indian losses at fifty or more, as the troops came on three burying holes that contained forty dead men within them.

The Cherokees managed to carry off much of their property and food from the village before the redcoats arrived. Montgomery was disappointed in the small amount of loot found at Etchoe compared to the butcher's bill his force suffered: "This one rather cost us too dear." Montgomery considered his losses (especially the number of wounded who needed care), the projected cost of continuing the march into the Middle Towns and the distance his men were from their base at Fort Prince George and decided to "return to march down the country and embark directly for [New] York." He convinced himself that he had complied with Amherst's orders and "succeeded in everything we have attempted." After two days at Etchoe, the British troops left during the night of June 30, in order to "get clear of the many dangerous passes near that town with our wounded and provisions" under cover of darkness. The men reached Fort Prince George within several days and then proceeded to Charles Town, assigning four companies of the First Regiment to remain at the Congarees. Many of the redcoats deserted the ranks as the army moved from Fort Prince George to Charles Town; the rest of the British soldiers sailed for New York.[181]

Despite the refusal of the assembly to pass a bill to support Montgomery's campaign against the Cherokees in 1760, North Carolina's governor tried to help. Dobbs "summoned the Assembly to meet at Wilmington" on June 26, "to try if the spreading of the Flame of war will induce them to give a supply and raise Men without Clogs or Delay now the storm approaches."[182] Several assemblymen from the northern counties hostile to Dobbs did not attend the assembly session, "hoping that we could not make up a Sufficient Number to do Business without them." The assembly

The rugged mountains of western North Carolina, in which British and colonial troops campaigned against the Cherokees in 1760 and 1761. *Author photo.*

nevertheless passed a measure to raise and pay three hundred men until December 1 and for issuing £12,000 in paper bills for military expenses. The bill also allowed the governor to send the troops out of the colony if necessary. Dobbs must have been relieved, but he warned Secretary Pitt that with Montgomery's departure from the Carolina frontier, "the Cherokee war is likely to be Bloody."[183]

As it turned out, the governor was correct in his predictions. In August, after reaching an agreement with the besieging Cherokees to allow his troops to depart Fort Loudoun unmolested, the British garrison's commander, Captain Demere, decided to abandon the stockade and march with his men and their dependents to Fort Prince George. After the garrison made camp beside Cane Creek fifteen miles from the fort, enemy Cherokees surrounded the British position and attacked the next morning. In the fighting that ensued, all of the garrison was either killed or captured, and Captain Demere lay dead.[184]

Although North Carolina's Assembly did not provide troops for Montgomery's 1760 campaign, many Carolinians were active that year in defending the colony's exposed frontier and fighting the Cherokees.

Legislative records include expenses allowed by the assembly for militia and ranging companies to keep watch in the backcountry as far back as 1757, but mostly for 1759 and 1760. For example, the house allowed ten pounds to Henry Harmon, "who went with a party under the command of Captain Teague," for "the taking of an Indian scalp." Jacob Lash was "allowed his claim of four pounds ten shillings and ten pence for dieting a party of scouting men, sent out by him, who has not charged anything for their time." He was "also allowed a claim of twelve pounds five shillings and four pence for four men scouting by his order on the frontiers for forty-six days." A company under Captain Gideon Wright was "allowed their claim for scouting fifty-two days" in April of 1760. Captain Thomas Donnol and his company were paid "for scouting five sundry times in the year 1760." Captain Griffith Rutherford, who would later gain fame as a North Carolina militia general during the Revolutionary War, commanded a ranging company that was "allowed their claim of one hundred and ninety-seven pounds two shillings, for scouting in March 1760."[185]

In addition to scouting, evidence shows that many backcountry Carolinians participated in what the assembly called "an expedition against the Cherokees" sanctioned by the colony in early 1760 and conducted by volunteers, not provincial soldiers. This was probably in support of Lyttelton's campaign of 1759. Numerous claims for expenses were honored by the assembly after the fact, "from the frontiers for services done on the expedition against the Cherokees, ranging companies, wagoning, etc." Although the existing correspondence of Arthur Dobbs makes no mention of this activity on the frontier, dozens of claims for expenses were nevertheless honored for that year and for "ranging" as well. In May 1760, for instance, the house allowed "that a proper allowance be made for the taking of ten Indian scalps…taken by a party of volunteers who went out at their own expense…to be equally divided amongst the adventurers in proportion to the number of scalps." The assembly's language does not describe the men as "soldiers," but as "volunteers" and "adventurers."[186]

The massacre of the Fort Loudoun garrison all but guaranteed a reprisal by South Carolina and British authorities, although they also sought opportunities for a peace agreement with the Cherokees. The new military expedition to the frontier planned for 1761 was to be led by Colonel James Grant, Abercromby's second in command during the previous campaign. By January 1761, Grant had arrived in Charles Town with a force made up of four companies of the Twenty-second and Seventeenth regiments totaling 340 men, several independent companies of redcoats recently shipped from England via New York numbering 800 soldiers (soon consolidated into Burton's Ninety-fifth Regiment), the four companies of the First (Royal) Regiment that had remained in South Carolina and a handful of friendly Indians.[187]

Before the troops marched west, Grant and his officers had to collect supplies, wagons, horses and cattle and muster the provincials. In addition, the campaign could not begin until there was sufficient grass in the woods for the horses, and the Indians' corn crop was sufficiently high to be destroyed. Grant and some South Carolinians doubted the ability of his forces to inflict an overwhelming defeat on the Cherokees in an operation so far from its logistical base and because the Cherokee towns were spread out in rugged terrain. General Amherst, however, pressed for action. "Punished…they must be," he wrote to Grant, "and that severely too, before Peace is granted them."[188]

In addition to the regulars sent south from New York to serve as the core of the army operating westward against the Cherokees, Amherst and other Crown authorities expected the southern colonies to support the campaign vigorously with their own troops and provisions. The plan for the campaign was to pressure the Cherokee towns from two directions. Grant's regulars—bolstered by South Carolina provincials—would march from the Low Country into the Middle Towns via forts Ninety-Six and Prince George, similar to Montgomery's campaign the previous year. Meanwhile, Virginia troops under Colonel William Byrd III were expected to move toward the Overhill Towns and attack them from the north, advancing from southwestern Virginia along the Holston River with hundreds of provincials into what is now eastern Tennessee.

This pincer movement may have appeared feasible on maps studied by British officers in far away New York, but commanders in the Carolinas and the Old Dominion must have seen its drawbacks right away. Coordination between the two forces would be almost impossible given the rugged terrain and great distances involved. Moreover, both elements would be far away from their sources of supply and reinforcement and would face challenging logistical difficulties in country where few settlements or farmsteads existed. As Virginia's legislature, the House of Burgesses, pointed out to Amherst in early 1761, Colonel Byrd's regiment could not possibly succeed against the Cherokees "when we consider the distance they must march, the difficulties of the country they must pass through, and the superior number of the enemy; which will, probably, be much increased by the Creeks, who may

During the Cherokee War of 1760–61, British and colonial forces struggled to operate in mountainous terrain like these peaks in frontier North Carolina. *Author photo.*

readily and, we fear, will willingly join them." Despite this warning, the campaign proceeded.[189]

Although peace negotiations between the Cherokees and Carolinians continued in 1761, Indians still raided white settlements, and preparations for the military campaign progressed. By late spring, Grant's force was in the backcountry with almost three thousand men, including a South Carolina provincial regiment (in which many North Carolinians served) under Colonel Thomas Middleton. By the end of May, the troops began to arrive at Fort Prince George, to prepare for their campaign in the mountains as they strengthened the fort.[190] They marched toward the Middle Cherokee towns on June 7 with enough supplies for one month, during which time Grant would make a "swift punishing raid," rather than conduct an extensive campaign.[191]

To the north, Virginia's efforts were hampered by a lack of provisions and supplies. While North Carolina was expected to assist Byrd's offensive, the Virginia colonel warned General Amherst not to expect much support from North Carolina based on the assembly's "preceding conduct." The Virginia House of Burgesses also advised Amherst that "we cannot hope for any assistance" from North Carolina in an address of March 1761. Amherst, however, maintained his expectations of North Carolina for the coming military operations. Although the general thought Byrd's regiment was adequate to the task of attacking the Overhill Towns, "this ought not…excuse the province of North Carolina, from furnishing her aid towards this essential & important service." He added, however, "I cannot say that I have much dependence on it." Byrd instead suggested that Amherst send five hundred regulars to southwestern Virginia for the operations he planned and informed Colonel Grant that his few troops were poorly equipped for the campaign, which they would begin from Augusta Courthouse.[192]

By July 1, the Virginia Regiment of over six hundred men had marched southward along the Great Warrior Path to Fort Chiswell (near modern Wytheville) on their way to Samuel Stalnaker's Plantation on the North Fork of the Holston River in southwestern Virginia (at today's Chilhowie). This was almost a month after Grant's troops had left Fort Prince George to move into Cherokee country and just eight days before these redcoats and South Carolinians returned to their camps. The earlier predictions that the campaign would be poorly coordinated had come true.[193]

In North Carolina, Dobbs had worked to get the colonial government to make some allowance for the southern operations of 1761, although it was unlikely, given past efforts, that any British leader in America looked for much help. "If Troops should be now required for carrying on any foreign expedition," Dobbs wrote, and "as the Assembly will meet the 20th of March, if they are in Temper, they may be raised and ready for action time enough yet for a summer campaign either against the Cherokees or French at Mississippi." Dobbs's optimism, however, was unfounded.[194]

The assembly did meet at the end of March. The lower house took up Secretary Pitt's circular letter asking the colony to "Continue the War with Vigour in America to drive the French from this Continent," though by this time Quebec and Montreal were both in British hands. Amherst also wrote Dobbs on January 19, 1761, with "strenuous" recommendations for aid. The general hoped that the troops could be raised in time to join the southern campaign. Amherst wrote that he

must therefore once more hope that the province of North Carolina will not have been backward in exerting themselves to their utmost, in aiding &

assisting in so essential a service, but that they will, as they ought, have cheerfully & speedily contributed…with all their might and capacity.

The assembly finally voted in April an "Aid of £20,000 Proclamation Money for raising[,] Cloathing and paying Five hundred effective Men exclusive of Officers to be Employed…in America," which Dobbs approved. Although he cannot have looked favorably on the printing of more paper money, he would no doubt have agreed with the assessment of North Carolina's James Murray (made several years beforehand) that the unsecured "paper Money [the assembly is] so bewitchingly fond of gives them, it is true, some temporary Relief, but certainly brings Discredit, Perfidy & Poverty in the Rear."[195]

The provincial force that the assembly voted to embody for the campaign against the Cherokees was organized into a regiment of five companies, each with one hundred men, who were to serve for seven months beginning on May 1, 1761. The troops were to participate with the Virginians of Byrd's regiment against the Overhill Towns in western North Carolina, although the assemblymen did note that it was "now too late in the season of the year for us to hope or expect men can be raised in time to be of any use in the present Expedition." Nevertheless, the governor tepidly thanked the assembly for "the supply Granted to his Majesty, an Aid upon this Critical situation of affairs and Poverty of this Province as great as could be expected to be raised in time to co-operate with the other regular and Provincial Troops."[196]

In South Carolina, Colonel Grant proceeded in June with his operations in the rugged western mountains through "impenetrable" country on "bad roads" and in heavy rains—knowing full well that the expected movements of the Virginia and North Carolina forces had not yet begun. After crossing into North Carolina on the morning June 10, Grant's regulars and the South Carolinians met a strong force of Cherokees before they reached the town of Etchoe, just beyond the site of the previous year's bloody battle. The line of march was "in a very narrow pass" between the Little Tennessee River to the west and steep mountain terrain on the east. Cherokee warriors fired from covered positions across the river and on the wooded slopes when the redcoats and provincials entered the pass, marching quickly to reach open ground and leave the dangerous kill zone. For several hours, the Indians fired down on the invaders from "amazingly advantageous" positions. The Indians also attacked the army's wagons in the rear, but Grant prudently sent back 175 South Carolinians to repulse the attackers.

The Little Tennessee River in North Carolina, near the site of Grant's 1761 victory over the Cherokees. *Author photo.*

To the front, the troops reached a ford of the river and forced their way across it. They also managed to occupy a hill on the opposite bank that allowed them to cover the crossing. Before noon, Grant's entire command had forded the river with its wagons, and the Indians withdrew as their ammunition supply began to run low.[197] With only light casualties after the battle, Grant moved his troops northward and eventually destroyed over eight hundred houses in fifteen towns, as well as their nearby crops and orchards, although the majority of Cherokee warriors had escaped. With his army exhausted and exposed, Grant marched it back to Fort Prince George by July 9 on difficult paths over steep mountains. In late August, Cherokee leaders were compelled to begin overtures to Grant and colonial officials for an eventual peace, which was concluded later that year.[198]

One of the South Carolina officers to serve with Colonel Grant on his foray against the Cherokee towns was Francis Marion, who would later gain considerable fame as the "Swamp Fox" during the American Revolution. Lieutenant Marion described the destruction of the Cherokee towns in

North Carolina shortly after the battle and was moved to sympathize with the plight of the defeated Indians:

> *We proceeded, by Colonel Grant's orders, to burn the Indian cabins. Some of the men seemed to enjoy this cruel work, laughing heartily at the flames, but to me it appeared a shocking sight. Poor creatures, thought I, we surely need not grudge you such miserable habitations. But when we came, according to our orders, to cut down the fields of corn, I could scarcely refrain from tears. Who, without grief, could see the stately stalks with broad green leaves and tasseled shocks, the staff of life, sink under our swords with all their precious load, to wither and rot untasted in their mourning fields.[199]*

Lieutenant Francis Marion, here depicted during the War of American Independence, served in the South Carolina Regiment during the Cherokee War in 1760. *Lossing*, Field-Book of the Revolution, *1859.*

Another officer also left a description of the army's advance through the steep hills and deep defiles of western North Carolina after the June 10 battle, "over some of the highest mountain[s] I ever saw." British army captain Christopher French of the Twenty-second Regiment recorded in his journal the movement of Grant's command and the destruction the soldiers wrought on the Cherokee villages they encountered. His entry for June 28 is typical. After burning a town and destroying crops early in the morning, the troops then marched to Tessuntee, on Cowee Creek near today's Franklin. Here, some of Grant's Indians brutally killed "an old Cherokee," after which they ran "a large stick down his throat, stuck an arrow into each of his sides, one into his neck and left a tomahawk sticking in his head." The soldiers destroyed the nearby corn and burned the town and then marched most of the day to Elajoy along the Little River, near modern Marysville, Tennessee. At this site, the troops "destroyed the corn and burned the town and marched from thence about half past two." Several hours later, after a fatiguing march in hot weather the soldiers reached a small village (the name of which Captain French did not record), where they encamped in a "pleasant dale." For several more days, the redcoats and provincials marched and burned as they came across Indian towns, fields and orchards while crossing "many steep mountains."[200]

Mountains of North Carolina in Cherokee Territory along the Little Tennessee River, in which Montgomery and Grant campaigned in 1760 and 1761. *Author photo.*

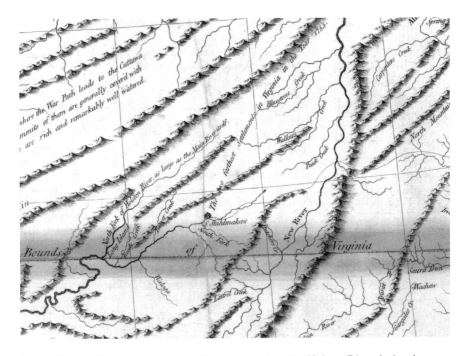

This 1778 map detail shows the area of operations along the Holston River during the Cherokee War. Colonel Waddell's North Carolina troops marched from "Wachaw" to Stalnakers and then down the Holston to Long Island in 1761. *North Carolina Collection, Wilson Library, UNC–Chapel Hill.*

While Grant marched, fought and wreaked havoc in western North Carolina, Colonel Byrd's Virginia troops arrived at Stalnaker's Plantation by July 12. Byrd was concerned that the warriors driven out of the Middle Towns by Grant's campaign now faced his own regiment as it drew closer to the Overhill Towns. He anticipated receiving some reinforcements from North Carolina at Long Island (also called Big Island) on the Holston River, at today's Kingsport, Tennessee, about sixty miles from Stalnaker's Plantation.

Frustrated by the delays caused in part by a lack of adequate supplies he received from contractors, Byrd resigned his commission in August. Command of the regiment fell on Lieutenant Colonel Adam Stephen, a longtime officer in the Virginia forces and a former physician. The following month, Stephen wrote to Colonel Waddell at Fort Dobbs, "requesting him to detach his recruits by companies to join the Virginia Regt. as soon as he could possibly get them armed & appointed."[201] By this time, Grant's troops had already destroyed the Middle Towns and were back in their camps in South Carolina.

Delays also hampered the movement of North Carolina troops to the far western frontier. On July 6, the governor ordered all available North Carolina provincial troops to join the Virginia Regiment serving on the Holston. The men were to rendezvous first at Fort Dobbs and then to "march, as many as are ready, by detachments, on the first notice from Colonel Byrd to Colonel Waddell."[202] By early October, Colonel Stephen had heard nothing from Waddell or any of his troops,[203] but the latter was not inactive. Waddell collected 374 men and 52 allied Indians at Salisbury, although he reported that he had no more than fifty stands of arms for the men. Accordingly, he "would use his endeavors to collect a sufficient number [of arms] through the province," probably by impressing weapons from the citizenry. Colonel Stephen was wary of the quality of these men, noting that "new raised men ill armed can but ill execute orders."[204]

On September 24, Waddell arrived at Bethabara with his men, prepared to march toward the New River. "The officers kept good order," reported the Moravians, "and the soldiers enjoyed our good, cheap bread." Before reaching Bethania a few miles away, some of the soldiers mutinied on the following day over having to serve outside of the colony. At their camp on Dorothea Creek, the officers "meted out punishment" to the mutineers, although none were executed. When the march resumed, "the officers left their best clothes, their papers, and money in our care until they should return."[205]

By early October, Waddell and the men he could gather and equip (and several dozen Tuscarora Indians) arrived at Fort Chiswell, three hundred strong and "willing to undertake anything."[206] By the end of the month, the North Carolina men had marched one hundred miles to join Colonel Stephen's force on the Holston. Their firelocks were in such poor shape that Stephen had to "employ armourers to repair arms for them." Still, he was impressed by the Carolina companies. "They behave extremely well for new raw troops," he observed, "and Colonel Waddell and the corps are so hearty in the service that we should have certainly attempted" to attack the Overhill Towns if circumstances had permitted.

Waddell commanded one of the five companies himself, the other four being led by Lieutenant Colonel Moore,[207] Major Bailie and Captains Richard Cogdell and Robert Howe. At Long Island, the Carolinians encamped by the newly erected Fort Robinson, named after John Robinson Jr., Virginia's

Left: Robert Howe served as a captain in the North Carolina forces on the Holston River campaign in 1761 and later as a general in the American Revolution. *Lossing,* Field-Book of the Revolution, *1859*.

Below: Long Island on the Holston River, near the site of Fort Robinson, at modern Kingsport, Tennessee. Provincial troops from Virginia and North Carolina halted their campaign here against the Cherokees in 1761. *William Jack photo.*

Speaker of the House of Burgesses. Stephen's men had constructed this stronghold of hewn logs, "with four bastions," on the north bank of the Holston, opposite the upper end of Long Island. This fort was "the only one advanced between Pittsburgh and Ft. Prince George," Stephen reported. Its walls were "sufficient in thickness to withstand the force of a small cannon shot," and "the gates were spiked with large nails so that the wood was entirely covered."[208]

A troop return from this camp on October 24 showed that Colonel Waddell's company included 1 officer, 3 sergeants, 4 boatmen, 4 servants, 34 Indians, 38 fit for duty and 2 sick. Moore's company had 2 officers, 2 sergeants, 6 servants and 38 men fit for duty. Major Baillie counted 1 sergeant and 28 soldiers fit for duty, and Captain Cogdell's company listed 21 fit for duty. Captain Howe's unit included 2 officers, 1 sergeant, 3 boatmen, 5 servants, 28 fit for duty and 1 man sick. This totaled 225 men under Waddell's overall command, far fewer than the 400 in the ranks at Bethabara one month earlier.[209]

The conclusion of the 1761 campaign on the Holston River was anticlimactic. The combined force of Virginians and North Carolinians saw no combat as the Cherokee conflict gradually came to an end by November. In late November, Waddell led the Carolinians and their Tuscarora auxiliaries back home, where they were disbanded at the Moravian towns. This was the last active military operation for North Carolina soldiers during the French and Indian War.[210]

Meanwhile, as Waddell and his officers had struggled to raise and equip their companies for service against the Cherokees during the summer and autumn of 1761, Governor Dobbs had tried to get the legislature to continue supporting the colony's forces in active service. Once the peace treaties between the Cherokees and the southern colonies seemed near to being finalized by the fall, he convened the assembly again, "in order to Know whether the whole Regiment should be disbanded" as well as "the Company that garrisoned the forts or what number should be thought proper to be kept on foot[,] as by the Law they were to be disbanded" on December 1. Dobbs ran into trouble with the Lower House over political issues and what constituted a quorum. "They Continued Obstinate," Dobbs complained to the Board of Trade, so he "let them Dissolve themselves; and next day Issued Writs for a New assembly returnable the 19th of June." As a consequence, all of the colony's troops were to be disbanded in the late fall, including the garrisons of the seacoast forts, although Dobbs did find sufficient funds available to maintain ten men and a gunner at Fort Johnston to guard the stores there.[211]

Doubtlessly discouraged by the assembly's refusal to keep the colony's troops on foot, Dobbs nevertheless must have been pleased that Fort Johnston on the Cape Fear River was nearly finished. He described it in 1761 as a "square fort with 4 Bastions with a dry Ditch and pallisaded Counterscarp," supported by "a large lower Battery upon the Counterscarp next [to] the River which commands the Channel at the Entrance of Cape Fear River." Most of the parapet was "made of what they call Tabby," a material "composed of Lime[,] Sand and Shells[,] which makes a strong Cement, there being no Stone but some Shelly Limestone within 100 miles of the Sea Coast." Once complete, the fort would also include barracks and a powder magazine, along with thirty guns, most of which had already been mounted on carriages. Until the assembly had disbanded the garrison, twenty men had been stationed there. By this time, the batteries at Ocracoke Bar and Topsail Inlet also had barracks but still no cannon, except "old Ship Guns."[212]

Although the Cherokee conflict had ended, Britain was still at war with France and, as such, continued to expect its colonies to assist in waging the contest. In February 1762, General Amherst called on North Carolina to provide recruits for his regular regiments, most of which were in the north. "The King has this Measure at heart," the general wrote to Dobbs, informing him of "how disagreeable any failure or Disappointment therein wod be to his Majesty." He called on North Carolina for 134 men, who were to be recruited by "five pounds New York Currency Bounty Money to each Man not under 18 nor above 40 years of Age who shall enlist to serve during this War, or until the Regiments return to Europe." In addition, the British army would clothe and pay the men, "without any further Expence to your Province." Officers would be allowed forty shillings for each man they recruited. This plan was to be presented to the colony's assembly for its support, Amherst advised.[213]

Amherst was not the only imperial official to press the colony for military help. Charles Wyndham, Earl of Egremont, became secretary of state for the Southern Colonies in October 1761, replacing William Pitt. The new secretary asked Dobbs to use his "influence, with the Council & Assembly of your Province, to induce them to raise…as large a Body of Men, as the Number of it's Inhabitant's may allow" to be prepared to move to any place in North America that the commander in chief ordered.[214]

When the assembly met in April 1762, Dobbs tried to convince the representatives to provide the troops called for by Amherst and Egremont. North Carolina's lower house, however, had other ideas. In a message to Dobbs, the Lower House reminded him:

We think the raising of Troops at this time, further than for the Defence of our Sea Coast, a Measure no-wise calculated to please the one, or

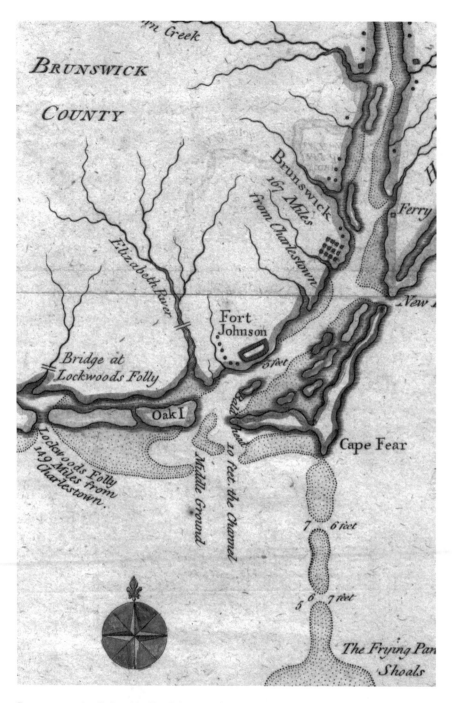

Postwar map detail showing Fort Johnston, Cape Fear and Brunswick. *North Carolina Collection, Wilson Library, UNC–Chapel Hill.*

benefit the other, for though we have the greatest Veneration for the best of Kings, and trust this Province has already given the most Convincing Proofs of its attachment to the Honor and Interest of the Crown, in the Prosecution of the present Just and necessary War; yet we are sorry to observe, that at this time, we cannot without reducing the Province to the utmost distress, consent to add to the accumulated and Intolerable Load of Taxes we are already Groaning under…the raising of Troops under our present Debility, must have a Tendency the most fatal to the Welfare and happiness of the Province, and drive the Inhabitants already impatient of their Sufferings, to the very brink of despair; and We beg leave to assure your Excellency, that from these Motives and these only, it is that we think ourselves unable to answer his Majesty's Expectations as expressed in the Letter laid before us, and we hope and earnestly request, your Excellency will be pleased to think so favourably of us, as not to impute our not complying with your Excellency's request to any other cause whatsoever.[215]

In what Dobbs called "a strong struggle," the delegates denied any meaningful assistance, so the governor dissolved the house "after repeated solicitations and short prorogations to reconsider and reflect upon their proceedings." Instead, "they were as obstinate as mules," in Dobbs's opinion. No bounty money was allowed in the house's recruiting proposal, which discouraged enlistment (and saved the colony money), and the number of men proposed was "not sufficient to defend the Forts." In addition, the assembly refused to authorize the recruiting of 134 men for service in Amherst's regulars. The French had for the most part been ejected from North America, and the Carolina frontier had quieted considerably by that point. No wonder, then, that cash-starved North Carolinians were through with raising money and men for British imperial designs. On his own initiative, the governor decided to "augment the garrisons by completing them to 65 men…so as to make the garrison of Fort Johnston 40 men." Even so, this was "too few for a Fort which holds our only Magazine and 30 Guns…besides Swivels." Dobbs advanced personal funds to "expedite the raising [of] the recruits and men for the Forts," in order to promote "His Majesty's service and the safety of the Province."[216]

By the end of 1762, the worldwide conflict later known as the Seven Years' War had moved far away from North Carolina. At the meeting of the colony's assembly that fall, Dobbs had to report that he had received

"no Instructions from His Majesty to require an aid for the Public Service."
The governor recommended only that the delegates raise money to provide
for contingencies, retire the colony's debts and support the garrisons of
the seacoast forts. The former conflicts Dobbs had fought with stubborn
and tightfisted assemblymen had eased, as his incessant demands for men,
money and supplies ended by the following year.[217] The lower house did,
perhaps grudgingly, recognize the propriety of some military expenses, even
as late as February 1764, including the need for a small force to man the forts
and guard the stores there. The delegates were pleased that no further call
for military aid came from the Crown or its ministers, "as the Province still
labours under a large debt occasioned by the many liberal grants made for
the service of the late war."[218]

For North Carolina's Indian allies and enemies, the war was devastating.
A powerful smallpox outbreak in 1759 reduced the Catawba population to
around five hundred people, including just one hundred warriors. This led
to their establishment of a smaller, consolidated settlement at Twelve Mile
Creek in South Carolina and a land reservation of fifteen square miles in
modern York and Lancaster counties. "They are now scarce a Nation but a
small village," Arthur Dobbs concluded in 1762. During the last days of the
war, a Shawnee war party killed the Catawba chief King Hagler in 1763, a
devastating blow to the Nation's morale and strength. By June of that year,
the Nation was reduced to only fifty warriors.[219]

When, in 1763, King George III approved a Proclamation Act barring
further settlement beyond the peaks of the Appalachian Mountains, in
theory Cherokee lands were safe from additional colonial encroachment.
In practice, however, white settlers and land speculators continued to
pressure the native people, resulting in further Cherokee land sessions in
1768, 1770, 1773 and 1775, involving perhaps fifty thousand square miles
of territory. In 1776, the Cherokees sided with Great Britain at the outbreak
of the Revolutionary War and began to attack Carolinians on the frontier. It
proved to be a costly decision, as an invasion of their land by Virginia, South
Carolina and North Carolina that year destroyed much of their property,
provisions and towns. They were also forced to cede significant portions of
their land as well.[220]

One of the more obvious signs that the war was over in North Carolina
was at the province's primary frontier stronghold, Fort Dobbs. At the end of
1761, while Waddell and most of the provincial soldiers were on their way
home from the Holston River, only thirty men were stationed at the fort. In
1763, "a half ton of lead from Fort Dobbs was traded to Gottfried Aust"

in the Moravian settlements for glazing pottery, since there was no further need to cast bullets at the fort. With no enemy to the west, no garrison was required, and the assembly compensated a caretaker for the fort in February 1764, Captain Walter Lindsey. "The fort was officially closed in March 1764, and the military stores ordered to Salisbury to save money." The fort was still marked on English maps of the colony made in 1770 and 1775, as well as a 1778 French map.[221]

Fort Johnston, however, was maintained by the colony, and an assembly committee inspected the fort and found it to be in good condition in 1764. Between its two batteries, there were still nine eighteen-pounders and nine nine-pounders. Other large guns lay scattered about the beach, unmounted. The committee also inspected "Nine Men fit for Duty, [who] appeared on the Platform." However, "the Tenth, they were informed deserted a few days before." In November 1764, the garrison consisted of only four men and an officer, Captain John Paine.[222]

CONCLUSION

From 1754 to 1761, North Carolina contributed to the British war efforts of the French and Indian War. This support diminished as the conflict progressed. The repeated demands for men and money from Dobbs, Pitt and British generals became too much for the assembly to bear, especially given the colony's financial straits. Moreover, there was no significant external military threat to North Carolina for much of the war, and when the Cherokees became openly hostile on the western frontier, the colony opted to support troops and fortifications in the South. Still, North Carolina troops served in three expeditions against Fort Duquesne, supported Loudoun's campaign in New York in 1756 and marched to the distant rivers of Tennessee against Indian foes in 1761. The province also built several forts on the coast and backcountry as well.

The war years were painful for the colony financially. Beginning in 1754, the assembly issued £72,000 in proclamation currency during the war years, in addition to £30,776 in treasury notes at 6 percent interest. North Carolina was reimbursed only £7,789 from the money set aside by Parliament for the southern colonies' war expenses. The assembly must have been glad by the end of the war to hear no more demands for aid to his Majesty every time they convened.[223]

The war years emboldened the assembly to assert colonial rights as well. Its members did not simply accede to British demands without debate, and by 1757, they made war aid contingent upon their own conditions. As we have seen, in 1759 the assembly voted no support at all, and at other legislative sessions, strings were attached to the military support it approved. In fact, the colony's greatest contribution to the war effort was in 1754, in numbers of men and amount of money never equaled during the conflict. Much of this was due to geographic and financial limitations, but a bigger issue had arisen as well, noted by Arthur Dobbs in late 1762. "It will be necessary," the governor wrote to General Amherst, "to have some British Force to Keep Down the rising Spirit of Independence." Dobbs was prescient: the Stamp Act crisis and its anti-British disturbances were only three years away.[224]

NOTES

Introduction

1. Anderson, *Crucible*, xv–xvi.
2. The quote is from Voltaire's satire *Candide*, published in 1759.

Chapter 1

3. Marsten, *Seven Years' War*, 7.
4. Titus, *Old Dominion*, 21.
5. Ibid., 30.
6. See Ekirch, *"Poor Carolina"* for an overview of the colony during the eighteenth century.
7. Nathaniel Rice to the Board of Trade of Great Britain, August 1, 1752, in Sanders, *Colonial Records of North Carolina*, 4:1314, and hereafter cited as *NCCR*.
8. August Gottlieb Spangenberg Journal, 1752–53, *NCCR*, 5:1–14.
9. Matthew Rowan to the Board of Trade, May 28, 1753, *NCCR*, 5:23–4.
10. Ibid., June 28, 1758, *NCCR*, 5:24.
11. Minutes of the North Carolina Governor's Council, March 12–19, 1756, *NCCR*, 5:655.
12. Arthur Dobbs to the Board of Trade of Great Britain, January 20, 1757, *NCCR*, 5:739–43. See also Merrell, *Indians' New World*.
13. Matthew Rowan to Robert D'Arcy, Earl of Holdernesse, November 21, 1753, *NCCR*, 5:25.

14. Board of Trade of Great Britain to Matthew Rowan, December 5, 1753, *NCCR*, 5:25–6.
15. Thomas Robinson, Baron Grantham, to Matthew Rowan, July 5, 1754, *NCCR*, 5:130–1.
16. Rowan to the Board of Trade, March 19, 1754, *NCCR*, 5:108–9.
17. Robert Dinwiddie to Thomas Robinson, Baron Grantham, June 18, 1754, *NCCR* 5:129.
18. Robert Dinwiddie to Matthew Rowan, March 23, 1754, *NCCR*, 5:110–11.
19. Return of William Gooch's Regiment (Extract), December 07, 1741, *NCCR*, 15:759; Lefler and Newsome, *North Carolina*, 154; James Murray to John Rutherford, March 3, 1755, North Carolina, Colonial Records.
20. Robert Dinwiddie to Matthew Rowan, March 23, 1754, *NCCR*, 5:110–11.
21. Robert Dinwiddie to James Innes, March 23, 1754, *NCCR*, 5:112.
22. Robert Dinwiddie to Matthew Rowan, April 15, 1754, *NCCR*, 5:118.
23. Commission of James Innes, *NCCR*, 5:125.
24. George Washington to Robert Dinwiddie, June 1754, *NCCR*, 5:128–9.
25. Matthew Rowan to the Board of Trade, June 3, 1754, *NCCR*, 5:123–4.
26. Ibid.
27. Horatio Sharpe to John Sharpe, April 19, 1755, *Correspondence of Governor Sharpe, 1753–1757*, Maryland, Correspondence; John Carlyle to George Washington, June 28, 1754, *George Washington Papers*, Library of Congress.
28. Robert Dinwiddie to James Innes, July 20, 1754, *NCCR*, 5:131–3.
29. Robert Dinwiddie to Thomas Robinson, Baron Grantham, September 23, 1754, *NCCR*, 11:122–3.
30. Ibid.
31. Maass, "North Carolina," 155–60.
32. Robert Dinwiddie to John Sharpe, September 5, 1754, *Correspondence of Governor Sharpe, 1753–1757*, Maryland, Correspondence; Robert Dinwiddie to Earl Granville, September 23, 1754, *NCCR*, 11:122.
33. Robert Dinwiddie to James Innes, July 20, 1754, *NCCR*, 5:131–3.
34. Robert Dinwiddie to Matthew Rowan, August 5, 1754, *NCCR*, 5:135–6.
35. Matthew Rowan to the Board of Trade, August 29, 1754, *NCCR*, 5:137.
36. Parkman, *Montcalm*, 95–6.
37. Matthew Rowan to the Board of Trade, October 22, 1754, *NCCR*, 5:144c–d; George Washington to John Carlyle, October 21, 1755, Fitzpatrick, *Writings*, 1:220; Nester, *First Global War*, 203.
38. Horatio Sharpe to Lord Calvert, September 15, 1754, *Correspondence of Governor Sharpe, 1753–1757*, Maryland, Correspondence; James Innes to

George Washington, August 11, 1754, *George Washington Papers*, Library of Congress; John Ridout to George Washington, August 27, 1754, *George Washington Papers*, Library of Congress, http://lcweb2.loc.gov/cgi-bin/query/r?ammem/mgw:@field(DOCID+@lit(lw010023)).

39. *Pennsylvania Gazette*, April 17, 1755.

Chapter 2

40. Petition from Arthur Dobbs concerning military fortifications in North Carolina, April 11, 1753, *NCCR*, 5:18–9.

41. Arthur Dobbs to the Board of Trade, November 9, 1754, *NCCR*, 5:144g–151.

42. Arthur Dobbs to the Earl of Halifax, November 20, 1754; *NCCR*, 5:157–60; Arthur Dobbs to John Campbell, Earl of Loudoun, July 10, 1756, *NCCR*, 5:594–601; Angley, *Fort Johnston*, 2.

43. Arthur Dobbs to Board of Trade, December 19, 1754, *NCCR*, 5:153–7.

44. Minutes of the Upper House of the North Carolina General Assembly, December 12–31, 1754, *NCCR*, 5:212–31.

45. Ibid.

46. John Clark to Matthew Rowan, September 25, 1754, *NCCR*, 5:140.

47. Report concerning the militia in each county of North Carolina, *NCCR*, 5:161–3.

48. Arthur Dobbs to [Thomas Robinson, Baron Grantham], January 1, 1755, *NCCR*, 5:312–13.

49. Arthur Dobbs to the Board of Trade, January 4, 1755, *NCCR*, 5: 314–20; Arthur Dobbs to the Board of Trade, February 8, 1755, *NCCR*, 5:330–4.

50. Peckham, *Colonial Wars*, 139–41.

51. Mullins, *Of Sorts*, 1–2, 11–12, 15.

52. Faragher, *Daniel Boone*, 36.

53. Robert Dinwiddie to Arthur Dobbs, February 8, 1755, *NCCR*, 5:367–8; ibid., April 30, 1755, *NCCR*, 5:400; Robert Dinwiddie to James Innes, May 1, 1755, *NCCR*, 5:401; Robert Dinwiddie to Arthur Dobbs, May 5, 1755, *NCCR*, 5:401-02; Wahl, *Braddock Road*, 42, 185; Pargellis, *Military Affairs*, 62.

54. "Memorandum from Arthur Dobbs to the Board of Trade of Great Britain concerning charges against him by the North Carolina General Assembly," 1760, *NCCR*, 6:280–310.

55. Wahl, *Braddock Road*, 190, 202, 231, 234, 248, 251, 255–56.

56. Ibid., 280–1; Pargellis, *Military Affairs*, 88–9.

57. Wahl, *Braddock Road*, 280–1.

58. Ibid., 375, 427; Swift, *Mid-Appalachian Frontier*, 30.

59. Horatio Sharpe to John Robinson, August 1755, *Correspondence of Governor Sharpe, 1753–1757*, Maryland, Correspondence.

60. Robert Dinwiddie to Arthur Dobbs, August 29, 1755, *NCCR*, 5:421–2.

61. Arthur Dobbs to the Board of Trade of Great Britain, August 24, 1755, *NCCR*, 5:353–64

62. Ibid.; Robert Dinwiddie to Arthur Dobbs, July 23, 1755, *NCCR*, 5:410.

63. The only biography of Hugh Waddell is Waddell, *Colonial Officer*.

64. Arthur Dobbs letter, August 25, 1755, *NCCR*, 5:419–20; Robert Dinwiddie to Arthur Dobbs, August 29, 1755, *NCCR*, 5:421–2; ibid., October 10, 1755, *NCCR*, 5:438.

65. Minutes of the Lower House of the North Carolina General Assembly, September 25 to October 15, 1755, *NCCR*, 5:524.

66. Arthur Dobbs to the Board of Trade, October 28, 1755, *NCCR*, 5:439–41.

67. Ibid., December 15, 1755, *NCCR*, 5:461–2.

68. Minutes of the North Carolina Governor's Council, August 28–29, 1755, *NCCR*, 5:491–2.

69. Upper House of the North Carolina General Assembly, September 25 to October 15, 1755, *NCCR*, 5:495–520

70. Arthur Dobbs to [Henry Fox, Baron Holland of Foxley], January 5, 1756, *NCCR*, 5:560.

71. Robert Dinwiddie to Arthur Dobbs February 5, 1756, *NCCR*, 5:561–2.

72. Arthur Dobbs to the Board of Trade, March 15, 1756, *NCCR*, 5:570–5.

73. Ibid.

74. Ibid.

75. Anderson, *War*, 95–6.

76. Arthur Dobbs to Henry Fox, March 26, 1756, *NCCR*, 5:576–7; Arthur Dobbs to Henry Fox, July 12, 1756, *NCCR*, 5:601–2; "Memorandum from Arthur Dobbs to the Board of Trade of Great Britain concerning charges against him by the North Carolina General Assembly," 1760, *NCCR*, 6:280–310; Sharpe to Calvert, May 5, 1756, *Correspondence of Governor Sharpe, 1753–1757*, Maryland, Correspondence; Arthur Dobbs Board of Trade, August 3, 1760, *NCCR*, 6:282–3.

77. *Pennsylvania Gazette*, May 20, 1756; ibid., June 10, 1756; ibid., June 17, 1756.

78. Arthur Dobbs to John Campbell, Earl of Loudoun, July 10, 1756, *NCCR*, 5:594–601.

79. "Memorandum from Arthur Dobbs to the Board of Trade of Great Britain concerning charges against him by the North Carolina General Assembly," 1760, *NCCR*, 6:280–310.

80. Anderson, *War*, 97–9, 106–7.

81. Anderson, *Crucible*, 150–7.

82. Anderson, *War*, 91–5; Pargellis, *Military Affairs*, 214–9, 187–93; Lord Loudoun to the Duke of Cumberland, August 20, 1756, in Pargellis, *Military Affairs*, 226; Benson and Toelke, *Waterways*, 20; Nelson, *Colonial New Jersey*, 20:49. See the *New York Mercury*, July 12, 1756. Thanks to Scott Lance for the reference to the *New York Mercury*.

83. Beverley Robinson to George Washington, July 23, 1759, Abbott, *Papers*, 3:285–9.

84. Robert Dinwiddie to Arthur Dobbs, September 18, 1756, *NCCR*, 5:610–1.

85. Arthur Dobbs to the Board of Trade, October 31, 1756, *NCCR*, 5:638–46; Lord Loudoun to the Duke of Cumberland, August 20, 1756, in Pargellis, *Military Affairs*, 223.

86. Lord Loudoun to the Duke of Cumberland, November 22, 1756, in Pargellis, *Military Affairs*, 267.

87. Arthur Dobbs to the Board of Trade, June 14, 1756, *NCCR*, 5:585–6; Order of the Privy Council of Great Britain, July 7, 1756, *NCCR*, 5:592–3; ibid.; Arthur Dobbs to Lord Loudoun, July 10, 1756, *NCCR*, 5:594–601.

88. Arthur Dobbs to Lord Loudoun, July 10, 1756, *NCCR*, 5:594–601.

89. Ibid.

90. Ibid.; Militia return and list of Taxables in North Carolina for the year 1755, including an account of ordnance, July 12, 1756, *NCCR*, 5:603–4.

91. Arthur Dobbs to Hugh Waddell, [Alexander Osborne], and Colonel Alexander, July 18, 1756, *NCCR*, 5:604–5; "Memorandum from Arthur Dobbs to the Board of Trade of Great Britain concerning charges against him by the North Carolina General Assembly," 1760, *NCCR*, 6:280–310.

92. Fries, *Records*, 1:164.

93. Ibid., 1:170; Melius, "Bathabara," 4–5. A copy of this manuscript was provided to me by Scott Douglas of Fort Dobbs State Historic Site.

94. Fries, *Records*, 1:170.

95. Arthur Dobbs to Henry Fox, October 30, 1756, *NCCR*, 5:638. The construction of the Catawba fort was started the next year but was not completed.

96. Arthur Dobbs to the Board of Trade, October 31, 1756, *NCCR*, 5:638–46.

97. Memorandum from James Abercromby to the Board of Trade of Great Britain concerning military aid from North Carolina, January 12, 1757, *NCCR*, 5:738–9.

Chapter 3

98. Circular letter from William Pitt, Earl of Chatham, to the American governors of the Southern Colonies, February 4, 1757, *NCCR*, 5:743–4.

99. Minutes of a meeting between Arthur Dobbs, et al., to plan for the defense of the southern colonies, March 15, 1757, *NCCR*, 5:750–2; Arthur Dobbs to the Board of Trade, March 22, 1757, *NCCR*, 5:753.

100. Arthur Dobbs to William Pitt, April 16, 1757, *NCCR*, 5:754–5.

101. Arthur Dobbs to the Board of Trade, May 30, 1757, *NCCR*, 5:761–4.

102. Ibid.

103. Robert Dinwiddie to John Campbell, Earl of Loudoun, July 9, 1757, *NCCR*, 5:767.

104. Minutes of the North Carolina Governor's Council, May 17–30, 1757, *NCCR*, 5:810–7.

105. Ibid.; *Fort Dobbs Gazette* 7, no. 2 (2010): 4 (a publication of the Fort Dobbs State Historic Site).

106. Fries, *Records*, 1:177–81.

107. Maass, "North Carolina," 155–60.

108. Minutes of the Lower House of the North Carolina General Assembly, May 16–28, 1757, *NCCR*, 5:843–68.

109. Dobbs to the Earl of Loudoun, July 10, 1756, *NCCR*, 5: 596–7; Babits and Pecoraro, "Fort Dobbs," part 2, 2005: 106. A copy of this report is at Fort Dobbs State Historic Site. Thanks to Larry Babits for assistance with this section of the book.

110. Minutes of the Lower House of the North Carolina General Assembly, May 16–28, 1757, *NCCR*, 5:843–68.

111. Minutes of the Upper House of the North Carolina General Assembly, November 21 to December 14, 1757, *NCCR*, 5:868–89.

112. William Pitt to Arthur Dobbs, December 30, 1757, *NCCR*, 5:789–91.

113. Arthur Dobbs to William Pitt, December 30, 1757, *NCCR*, 5:792–3.

114. John Campbell, Earl of Loudoun, to Arthur Dobbs, February 13, 1758, *NCCR*, 5:925–6.

115. Maass, "'All This Poor Province Could Do,'" 50–89.

Chapter 4

116. Hughes, *Siege of Fort William Henry*, 219–35.

117. William Pitt to Arthur Dobbs, December 30, 1757, *NCCR*, 5:789–91. The most recent, detailed account of the 1758 Forbes expedition is Cubbison, *Forbes Campaign*.

118. John Forbes to Arthur Dobbs, March 21, 1758, *NCCR*, 5:926–7.

119. Arthur Dobbs to the Board of Trade, April 30, 1758, *NCCR*, 5:932–3; Arthur Dobbs to William Pitt, May 7, 1758, *NCCR*, 5:934–5.

120. "Report by the Committee of both Houses of the North Carolina General Assembly Concerning Public Claims," December 19, 1758, *NCCR*, 5:977.

121. Arthur Dobbs to the Board of Trade April 30, 1758, 5:932–3; Arthur Dobbs to William Pitt, May 7, 1758, *NCCR*, 5:934–5; Ibid., March 19, 1759, *NCCR*, 6:17–8.

122. Minutes of the Lower House of the North Carolina General Assembly, April 28 to May 4, 1758, *NCCR*, 5:998–1012.

123. Maass, "'All This Poor Province Could Do,'" 59–60; Waddell and Bomberger, *French and Indian War*, 36.

124. Miller, "Fort Frederick's Role," 62–3; Horatio Sharpe to Francis Fauquier, July 12, 1758, in Reese, *Official Papers*, 1:51–2.

125. Kummerow, O'Toole and Stephenson, *Pennsylvania's Forbes Trail*, 93.

126. Maass, "'All This Poor Province Could Do,'" 60; Nester, *Great Frontier War*, 153.

127. Forbes quotes are from Leach, *Roots*, 131.

128. Maass, "'All This Poor Province Could Do,'" 60; Nester, *Great Frontier War*, 153.

129. Kummerow, *Pennsylvania's Forbes Trail*, 122; Chartrand, *Tomahawk*, 49–59.

130. George Washington to Francis Fauquier, September 25, 1761, Reese, *Official Papers*, 1:79–80.

131. Ibid., 1:81–2.

132. Ibid., September 2, 1758, Reese, *Official Papers*, 1:66.

133. Waddell and Bomberger, *French and Indian War*, 43, 53, 90; Anderson, *Crucible*, 273.

134. Waddell and Bomberger, *French and Indian War*, 53–5.

135. Kummerow, O'Toole and Stephenson, *Pennsylvania's Forbes Trail*, 142–3, 145; Chartrand, *Tomahawk*, 60–9.

136. John Forbes to Francis Fauquier, November 5, 1761, Reese, *Official Papers*, 1:100. Forbes actually wrote "South Carolina," but since he did not have troops from that province, he must have meant North Carolina.

137. Anderson, *Crucible*, 282–3; "Memorandum from Arthur Dobbs to the Board of Trade of Great Britain concerning charges against him by the North Carolina General Assembly," 1760, *NCCR*, 6:280–310.

138. Minutes of the Lower House of the North Carolina General Assembly, April 24 to May 23, 1760, *NCCR*, 6:362–420.

139. Minutes of the Lower House of the North Carolina General Assembly, April 24 to May 23, 1760, *NCCR*, 6:362–420; "Memorandum from Arthur Dobbs to the Board of Trade of Great Britain concerning charges against him by the North Carolina General Assembly," 1760, *NCCR*, 6:280–310; George Washington to Francis Fauquier, November 28, 1758, Reese, *Official Papers*, 1:115.

140. William Pitt to Southern Governors, December 9, 1758, Reese, *Official Papers*, 1:128–9.

141. Arthur Dobbs to William Pitt, April 11, 1759, *NCCR*, 6:24–5.

142. Dobbs to the Board of Trade of Great Britain, May 18, 1759, *NCCR*, 6:32–4; Arthur Dobbs to William Pitt, May 18, 1759, *NCCR*, 6:40–1; Maass, "'All this Poor Province Could Do,'" 65.

Chapter 5

143. Oliphant, *Peace and War*, 1–8; Lee, *Indian Wars*, 57.

144. Hatley, *Dividing Paths*, 80–5.

145. Oliphant, *Peace and War*, 21–2. The Catawbas were also a party to this treaty.

146. Hatley, *Dividing Paths*, 75–80, 92–5.

147. Ibid., 100–1, 105–15; Oliphant, *Peace and War*, 31–69; Peckham, *Colonial Wars*, 201–5; George Washington, "Instructions for Lieutenant James Roy," Fitzpatrick, *Writings*, 2:149–50.

148. Oliphant, *Peace and War*, 29–30.

149. Francis Fauquier to John Forbes, Reese, *Official Papers*, 1:52; George Washington to Francis Fauquier, July 20, 1758, Reese, *Official Papers*, 1:52–3; John Forbes to Francis Fauquier, August 16, 1761, Reese, *Official Papers*, 1:59–60.

150. Hatley, *Dividing Paths*, 100–1, 105–15; Oliphant, *Peace and War*, 31–69; Peckham, *Colonial Wars*, 201–5; George Washington, "Instructions for Lieutenant James Roy," Fitzpatrick, *Writings*, 2:149–50.

151. Fries, *Records*, 1:188–190, 206; Minutes of the Lower House of the North Carolina General Assembly, April 28, to May 4, 1758, *NCCR*, 5:1010.

152. Oliphant, *Peace and War*, 72–3; Amherst to Francis Fauquier, Reese, *Official Papers*,2:465; Eaker, *German Speaking*, 23.

153. Nathan Alexander to Governor Lyttelton, May 4, 1759, in McDowell, *Colonial Records*.

154. Fries, *Records*, 1:210–1.

155. Eaker, *German Speaking*, 23.

156. *Fort Dobbs Gazette* 7, no. 2 (June 2010): 5.

157. Jeffrey Amherst to John Robinson, March 25, 1761, Reese, *Official Papers*, 2:500.

158. Arthur Dobbs to William Pitt, October 14, 1759, *NCCR*, 6:60–62.

159. Ibid.

160. Hatley, *Dividing Paths*, 119–25; Arthur Dobbs to William Pitt, January 21, 1760 6:220–1; Nester, *First Global War*, 193.

161. Hugh Waddell to William H. Lyttelton, January 1, 1760, William Henry Lyttelton Papers, Box 14, William Clements Library, University of Michigan. Thanks to Daniel J. Tortora for providing this citation.

162. Arthur Dobbs to William Pitt, January 21, 1760, *NCCR*, 6:220–1.

163. Nester, *First Global War*, 193–4; Kelley, *Historic Fort*, 28–33.

164. Hugh Waddell to Arthur Dobbs [Extract] February 29, 1760, *NCCR*, 6:229–30.

165. Ibid.; *Fort Dobbs Gazette* 6, no. 4 (2010): 5.

166. Hatley, *Dividing Paths*, 127–8.

167. Fries, *Records*, 1:227, 229.

168. Ibid., 230–2.

169. Abraham Maury to Francis Fauquier, March 28, 1760, Reese, *Official Papers*, 1:339.

170. Nester, *First Global War*, 194; Jeffrey Amherst to Archibald Montgomery, February 24, 1760, in Mays, *Amherst Papers*, 79–80.

171. Arthur Dobbs to William Pitt, April 12, 1760, *NCCR* 6:234.

172. Arthur Dobbs to the Board of Trade May 28, 1760, *NCCR*, 6:243–51; Arthur Dobbs to William Pitt, May 29, 1760, *NCCR*, 6:257–9.

173. Arthur Dobbs to William Pitt, May 29, 1760, *NCCR*, 6:257–9; Nester, *First Global War*, 194.

174. Jeffrey Amherst to Archibald Montgomery, March 6, 1760, Mays, *Amherst Papers*, 81–4; Jeffrey Amherst to James Grant, March 8, 1760, Mays, *Amherst Papers*, 87.

175. Mays, *Amherst Papers*, 88–9.

176. Archibald Montgomery to Jeffrey Amherst, May 24, 1760, Mays, *Amherst Papers*, 104–8.

177. Ibid., June 4, 1760, Mays, *Amherst Papers*, 121–123.

178. Oliphant, *Peace and War*, 123–31; Archibald Montgomery to Jeffrey Amherst, July 2, 1760, Mays, *Amherst Papers*, 127–9.

179. Oliphant, *Peace and War*, 130–1; Archibald Montgomery to Jeffrey Amherst, July 2, 1760, Mays, *Amherst Papers*, 127–129.

180. Quote is given in Hatley, *Dividing Paths*, 131.

181. Mays, *Amherst Papers*, 130; Archibald Montgomery to Amherst, July 2, 1760, Mays, *Amherst Papers*, 127–9; ibid., August 15, 1760, Mays, *Amherst Papers*, 130–2.

182. Arthur Dobbs to William Pitt, June 14, 1760, *NCCR*, 6:263–4.

183. Ibid., July 21, 1760, *NCCR*, 6:266–7.

184. Nester, *First Global War*, 193–4; Kelley, *Historic Fort Loudoun*, 28–33; Oliphant, *Peace and War*, 136–9.

185. "Report by the Committee of both Houses of the North Carolina General Assembly Concerning Public Claims," December 3, 1760, *NCCR*, 22:824–7.

186. "Report by the Committee of both Houses of the North Carolina General Assembly Concerning Public Claims," May 20, 1760, *NCCR*, 22:818–23.

187. Oliphant, *Peace and War*, 140–4.

188. Ibid.

189. Address from the House of Burgesses to General Amherst, March 12, 1761, Reese, *Official Papers*, 2:487.

190. Oliphant, *Peace and War*, 140–53.

191. Ibid., 158.

192. William Byrd to Jeffrey Amherst, March 11, 1761, Mays, *Amherst Papers*, 206–8; William Byrd to James Grant, April 22, 1761, Mays, *Amherst Papers*, 241–42; James Grant to Jeffrey Amherst, June 2, 1761, Mays, *Amherst Papers*, 266–8; Address from the House of Burgesses to General Amherst, March 12, 1761, Reese, *Official Papers*, 2:487; Jeffrey Amherst to John Robinson, March 25, 1761, Reese, *Official Papers*, 2:501.

193. William Byrd to Jeffrey Amherst, March 11, 1761, Mays, *Amherst Papers*, 206–8; William Byrd to James Grant, April 22, 1761, Mays, *Amherst Papers*, 241–2; James Grant to Jeffrey Amherst, June 2, 1761, Mays, *Amherst Papers*, 266–8; Address from the House of Burgesses to General Amherst, March 12, 1761, Reese, *Official Papers*, 2:487; Jeffrey

Amherst to John Robinson, March 25, 1761, Reese, *Official Papers*, 2:501.

194. Arthur Dobbs to John Pownall, February 9, 1761, *NCCR*, 6:520–2.

195. Minutes of the Upper House of the North Carolina Assembly March 31 to April 23, 1761, *NCCR*, 6:638–61; Jeffrey Amherst to Francis Fauquier, Reese, *Official Papers*, 2:465; Jeffrey Amherst to Arthur Dobbs, January 19, 1761, Reese, *Official Papers*, 2:466–7; James Murray to John Rutherford, March 3, 1755, North Carolina, Colonial Records Project.

196. Minutes of the Lower House of the North Carolina Assembly, March 31 to April 23, 1761, *NCCR*, 6:661–97.

197. James Grant to Jeffrey Amherst, July 10, 1761, Mays, *Amherst Papers*, 277–80; Oliphant, *Peace and War*, 159–161.

198. James Grant to Jeffrey Amherst, July 10, 1761, Mays, *Amherst Papers*, 277–80; Oliphant, *Peace and War*, 162–3; Anderson, *Crucible*, 466; French, "Journal," 275–96.

199. Marion, "Sowing," 333.

200. French, "Journal," 288.

201. William Byrd to Jeffrey Amherst, August 2, 1761, Mays, *Amherst Papers*, 289–90; Jeffrey Amherst to William Byrd, August 17, 1761, Mays, *Amherst Papers*, 291–2; William Byrd to Jeffrey Amherst, September 7, 1761, Mays, *Amherst Papers*, 303–4; Adam Stephen to Jeffrey Amherst, October 5, 1761, Mays, *Amherst Papers*, 310–1.

202. Jeffrey Amherst to Francis Fauquier, August 2, 1761, Reese, *Official Papers*, 2:554–55.

203. William Byrd to Jeffrey Amherst, August 2, 1761, Mays, *Amherst Papers*, 289–90; Jeffrey Amherst to William Byrd, August 17, 1761, Mays, *Amherst Papers*, 291–2; William Byrd to Jeffrey Amherst, September 7, 1761, Mays, *Amherst Papers*, 303–4; Adam Stephen to Jeffrey Amherst, October 5, 1761, Mays, *Amherst Papers*, 310–1.

204. Adam Stephen to Francis Fauquier, August 2, 1761, Reese, *Official Papers*, 2:569.

205. Fries, *Records*, 237.

206. Adam Stephen to Francis Fauquier, October 8, 1761, Reese, *Official Papers*, 2:582-83; Francis Fauquier to Jeffrey Amherst, October 26, 1761, Reese, *Official Papers*, 2:588; *Fort Dobbs Gazette* 8, no. 2 (June 2011): 5.

207. Colonel Moore was possibly James Moore, who later served in the 1776 Moores Creek Bridge Campaign during the American Revolution.

208. Adam Stephen to Jeffrey Amherst, October 24, 1761, Mays, *Amherst Papers*, 323–4; Summers, *History*, 71; Nance, "Fort Patrick Henry." Hatley,

in *Dividing Paths*, 139, incorrectly identifies the fort as Fort Henry, a fort built in 1776 on the same site as Fort Robinson.

209. Enclosure in Adam Stephen to Jeffrey Amherst, October 24, 1761, "A Return of a Detachment of the North Carolina Regiment Encamped at Bigg Island on Houlstons River 23d October 1761," Amherst Papers, WO 34/47, folio 287. Thanks to Daniel J. Tortora for this citation.

210. Fries, *Records*, 234; Adam Stephen to Jeffrey Amherst, November 24, 1761, Amherst Papers, WO 34/40, folio 99. Thanks to Daniel J. Tortora for this citation.

211. Arthur Dobbs to the Board of Trade December 1761, *NCCR*, 6:596–600; Maass, "'All This Poor Province Could Do,'" 82.

212. Report by Arthur Dobbs concerning general conditions in North Carolina, 1761, *NCCR*, 6:605–23.

213. Jeffrey Amherst to Arthur Dobbs February 21, 1762, *NCCR*, 6:705–6.

214. Letter from Charles Wyndham, Earl of Egremont to Arthur Dobbs, December 12, 1761, *NCCR*, 6:592–4.

215. Minutes of the Lower House of the North Carolina General Assembly April 13–19, 1762, *NCCR*, 6:800–12.

216. Arthur Dobbs to Charles Wyndham, Earl of Egremont, April 30, 1762, *NCCR*, 6:712–3; Arthur Dobbs to the Board of Trade of Great Britain, April 30, 1762, *NCCR*, 6:713–4.

217. Minutes of the Upper House of the North Carolina General Assembly, November 3 to December 11, 1762, *NCCR*, 6:838–92.

218. Minutes of the Lower House of the North Carolina General Assembly, February 3 to March 10, 1764, *NCCR*, 6:1150–218.

219. Arthur Dobbs to Philip Bearcroft, April 15, 1760, *NCCR*, 6:235; Minutes of the North Carolina Governor's Council, December 4–31, 1762, *NCCR*, 6:787; Arthur Dobbs to the Board of Trade, June 17, 1763, *NCCR*, 6:989.

220. For details on the Cherokee conflict with the American colonies and Great Britain during this period, see Cashion, "North Carolina."

221. Babits and Pecoraro, "Fort Dobbs," 20–21.

222. Minutes of the Upper House of the North Carolina General Assembly, February 3 to March 10, 1764, *NCCR*, 6:1113.

Conclusion

223. Connor, *North Carolina*, 1:262–3.

224. Harry Ward, *"Unite"*, 120.

Bibliography

Abbott, William W., ed. *The Papers of George Washington, Colonial Series*. 10 vols. Charlottesville: University Press of Virginia, 1983–1995.

Anderson, Fred. *Crucible of War: The Seven Years' War and the Fate of Empire in British North America, 1754–1766*. New York: Alfred Knopf, 2000.

———. *The War That Made America: A Short History of the French and Indian War*. New York: Viking, 2005.

Angley, Wilson. *A History of Fort Johnston on the Lower Cape Fear River*. Southport, NC: Southport Historical Society, 1996.

Babits, Larry, and Tiffany A. Pecoraro. "Fort Dobbs, 1756–1763: Iredell County, North Carolina: An Archaeological Study," 2005.

———. "Fort Dobbs, 1756–1763: Iredell County, North Carolina: An Archaeological Study," 2008.

Benson, Steve, and Ron Toelke. *Waterways of War: The Struggle for Empire 1754–1763; A Traveler's Guide to the French & Indian War Forts and Battlefields along America's Byways in New York and Pennsylvania*. Sackets Harbor, NY: Seaway Trail, 2009.

Cashion, Jerry C. "North Carolina and the Cherokee: The Quest for Land on the Eve of the American Revolution, 1754–1776." Ph.D. dissertation, University of North Carolina, 1979.

Chartrand, Rene. *Tomahawk and Musket: French and Indian Raids in the Ohio Valley 1758*. Oxford, UK: Osprey, 2012.

Connor, R.D.W. *North Carolina: Rebuilding and Ancient Commonwealth*. 4 vols. Chicago: American Historical Society, 1928.

Cubbison, Douglas R. *The British Defeat of the French in Pennsylvania, 1758: A Military History of the Forbes Campaign Against Fort Duquesne.* Jefferson, NC: McFarland, 2010.

Eaker, Lorena S., ed. *German Speaking People West of the Catawba River in North Carolina, 1750–1800.* Church Hill, TN: SCK Publications, 1994.

Ekirch, A. Roger. *"Poor Carolina": Politics and Society in Colonial North Carolina, 1729–1776.* Chapel Hill: University of North Carolina Press, 1981.

Faragher, John M. *Daniel Boone: The Life and Legend of an American Pioneer.* New York: Henry Holt, 1992.

Fisher, George Park. *The Colonial Era.* New York: Charles Scribner's Sons, 1892.

Fitzpatrick, John C., ed. *The Writings of George Washington from The Original Manuscript Sources, 1745–1799.* 39 vols. Washington, D.C.: U.S. Government Printing Office, 1931–44.

Fort Dobbs Gazette, no. 2 (2010).

Fort Dobbs Gazette, no. 4 (2010).

Fort Dobbs Gazette, no. 2 (2011).

French, Christopher. "Journal of an Expedition to South Carolina," *Journal of Cherokee Studies* 2 (1977): 275–296.

Fries, Adelaide L. *Records of the Moravians in North Carolina.* Raleigh, NC: Edwards and Broughton, 1925.

George Washington Bicentennial Commission. *History of the George Washington Bicentennial Celebration,* Literature Series. 5 vols. Washington D.C., 1932.

The George Washington Papers at the Library of Congress. http://lcweb2.loc.gov/cgi-bin/query/r?ammem/mgw:@field(DOCID+@lit(lw010015)) (accessed April 1, 2013).

Hatley, Tom. *The Dividing Paths: Cherokees and South Carolinians through the Revolutionary Era.* New York: Oxford University Press, 1995.

Hughes, Ben. *The Siege of Fort William Henry: A Year on the Northeastern Frontier.* Yardley, PA: Westholme, 2011.

Kelley, Paul. *Historic Fort Loudoun.* Vonore, TN: Fort Loudoun Association, 1958.

Kummerow, Burton K., Christine H. O'Toole and R. Scott Stephenson. *Pennsylvania's Forbes Trail.* Lantham, MD: Taylor Trade Publishing, 2008.

Leach, Douglas E. *Roots of Conflict: British Armed Forces and Colonial Americans, 1677–1763.* Chapel Hill: University of North Carolina Press, 1986.

Lee, E. Lawrence. *Indian Wars in North Carolina, 1663–1763.* Raleigh: Carolina Tercentenary Commission, 1963.

Lefler, Hugh T., and Albert R. Newsome. *North Carolina: The History of a Southern State.* Chapel Hill: University of North Carolina Press, 1963.

Lossing, Benson John. *Harper's Encyclopedia of United States History from 458 A.D. to 1912*. New York and London: Harper Bros., 1912.

———. *The Pictorial Field-Book of the Revolution*. New York: Harper & Bros., 1859.

Lowdermilk, William H. *History of Cumberland (Maryland)*. Washington, D.C.: J. Anglim, 1878.

Maass, John R. "'All This Poor Province Could Do': North Carolina and the Seven Years' War, 1757–1762." *North Carolina Historical Review* 79 (2002): 50–89.

———. "North Carolina and the Seven Years' War, 1754–1758," *Military Collector and Historian* 55 (2003): 155–160.

Marion, Francis. "Sowing Tares of Hate," *Journal of Cherokee Studies* 2 (1977): 333.

Marsten, Daniel. *The Seven Years' War*. Oxford, UK: Osprey, 2001.

Maryland State Archives. Correspondence of the Governor. Archives of Maryland Online. http://aomol.net/megafile/msa/speccol/sc2900/sc2908/000001/000006/html/am6--196.html (accessed April 1, 2013).

Mays, Edith, ed. *Amherst Papers, 1756–1763: The Southern Sector*. Bowie, MD: Heritage Books, 1999.

McDowell, William L., Jr., ed. *Colonial Records of South Carolina, Series 2: Documents Relating to Indian Affairs, 1754–1765*. Columbia: South Carolina Archives Department, 1970.

Melius, Jason. "Bathabara: Native Relations, 1752–1774," n.d., copy at Fort Dobbs State Historic Site.

Merrell, James H. *The Indians' New World: Catawbas and Their Neighbors from European Contact Through the Era of Removal*. New York: W.W. Norton, 1991.

Miller, David P. "Fort Frederick's Role in the French and Indian War." Master's thesis, Shippensburg University, 1995.

Mullins, Jim. *Of Sorts for Provincials: American Weapons of the French and Indian War*. Elk River, MN: Track of the Wolf, 2008.

Nance, Benjamin. "Fort Patrick Henry." Tennessee Encyclopedia of History and Culture. http://tennesseeencyclopedia.net/entry.php?rec=493 (accessed March 15, 2013).

Nelson, William, ed. *Documents Relating to the Colonial History of the State of New Jersey*. Paterson, NJ: Call Printing and Publishing Co., 1898.

Nester, William R. *The First Global War: Britain, France, and the fate of North America, 1756–1775*. Westport, CT: Praeger, 2000.

———. *The Great Frontier War: Britain, France, and the Imperial Struggle for North America, 1607–1755*. Westport, CT: Praeger, 2000.

New York Mercury, July 12, 1756.

North Carolina Office of Archives and History. *The Colonial Records Project. Out of Print Bookshelf.* http://www.ncpublications.com/colonial/Bookshelf/murray/chap2.htm (accessed January 31, 2013).

Oliphant, John. *Peace and War on the Anglo-Cherokee Frontier, 1756–63*. Baton Rouge: Louisiana State University Press, 2001.

Pargellis, Stanley, ed. *Military Affairs in North America, 1748–1765*. New York: Appleton-Century Co., 1936.

Parkman, Francis. *Montcalm and Wolfe*. New York: DeCapo Press, 1995.

Peckham, Howard H. *The Colonial Wars, 1689–1762*. Chicago: University of Chicago Press, 1964.

Pennsylvania Gazette, April 17, 1755.

Reese, George, ed. *The Official Papers of Francis Fauquier, 1758–1768*. 3 vols. Charlottesville: University of Virginia Press, 1980–83.

Sanders, William L., ed. *The Colonial Records of North Carolina*. 10 vols. Raleigh, NC: P.M. Hale, State Printer, 1886–90.

Summers, Lewis P. *History of Southwest Virginia, 1746–1786...* Richmond, VA: J.L. Hill Printing Co., 1903.

Swift, Robert B. *The Mid-Appalachian Frontier: A Guide to Historic Sites of the French and Indian War*. Gettysburg, PA: Thomas Publications, 2001.

Titus, James. *The Old Dominion at War: Society, Politics, and Warfare in Late Colonial Virginia*. Columbia: University of South Carolina Press, 1991.

Waddell, Alfred M. *A Colonial Officer and His Times: A Biographical Sketch of Hugh Waddell of North Carolina*. Raleigh, NC: Edwards and Broughton, 1890.

Waddell, Louis M. and Bruce Bomberger, *The French and Indian War in Pennsylvania, 1753–1763: Fortification and Struggle During the War for Empire*. Harrisburg: Pennsylvania Historical and Museum Commission, 1996.

Wahl, Andrew J. *Braddock Road Chronicles, 1755*. Bowie, MD: Heritage Books, 1999.

Ward, Harry. *"Unite or Die": Intercolony Relations, 1690–1763*. Port Washington, NY: National University Publications, 1971.

William Henry Lyttelton Papers, Box 14, William L. Clements Library, University of Michigan.

INDEX

W

Y

ABOUT THE AUTHOR

John R. Maass grew up in the Shenandoah Valley, near Lexington, Virginia. He was the founder of the Rockbridge Civil War Round Table in 1981. He received a BA in history from Washington and Lee University in 1987, an MA in American history from the University of North Carolina at Greensboro in 2002 and a PhD in early U.S. history from the Ohio State University in 2007. Formerly a U.S. Army Reserve officer in the Transportation Corps, he is now a historian at the U.S. Army Center of Military History in Washington, D.C. He serves on the editorial staff of the *Journal of Backcountry Studies* and is currently working on a book about the military history of North Carolina for Westholme Press, due to appear in 2015. He lives near Mount Vernon, Virginia, with his wife and two children.